Collins

Aiming for Level
Speaking and
Listening

4

Keith Brindle

Nigel Carlisle

Janine Clatworthy

Steve Eddy

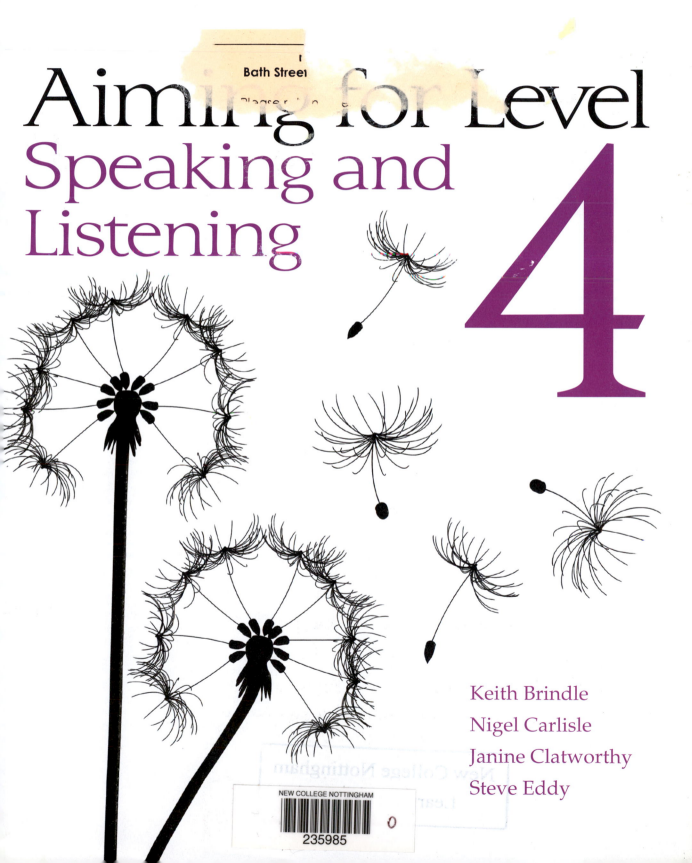

William Collins' dream of knowledge for all began with the publication of his first book in 1819. A self-educated mill worker, he not only enriched millions of lives, but also founded a flourishing publishing house. Today, staying true to this spirit, Collins books are packed with inspiration, innovation and practical expertise. They place you at the centre of a world of possibility and give you exactly what you need to explore it.

Collins. Freedom to teach.

Published by Collins Education
An imprint of HarperCollins Publishers
77-85 Fulham Palace Road
Hammersmith
London
W6 8JB

Browse the complete Collins Education catalogue at
www.collinseducation.com

© HarperCollins Publishers Limited 2011

10 9 8 7 6 5 4 3 2 1
ISBN 978 0 00 741592 2

Keith Brindle, Nigel Carlisle, Janine Clatworthy and Steve Eddy assert their moral rights to be identified as the authors of this work.

British Library Cataloguing in Publication Data.
A Catalogue record for this publication is available from the British Library.

Commissioned by Catherine Martin
Edited and project-managed by Sue Chapple
Design by Jordan Publishing Design Limited
Cover design by Angela English

With thanks to Caroline Green.

Mixed Sources
Product group from well-managed forests and other controlled sources
www.fsc.org Cert no. SW-COC-001806
© 1996 Forest Stewardship Council

FSC is a non-profit international organisation established to promote the responsible management of the world's forests. Products carrying the FSC label are independently certified to assure consumers that they come from forests that are managed to meet the social, economic and ecological needs of present and future generations.

Find out more about HarperCollins and the environment at
www.harpercollins.co.uk/green

Acknowledgements

The publishers gratefully acknowledge the permission granted to reproduce the copyright material in this book. While every effort has been made to trace and contact copyright holders, where this has not been possible the publishers will be pleased to make the necessary arrangements at the first opportunity.

p26 extract from an interview with Dame Ellen MacArthur by Barney Ronay. Courtesy of *The Guardian* 2008
p34 'Nooligan' by Roger McGough, from *In the Glassroom* © Roger McGough 1976. Reprinted by permission of United Agents.
p44 'The Landlady' by Roald Dahl, from *A Roald Dahl Selection* © Roald Dahl, 1959. Courtesy of David Higham Associates.
p53 'Waash'in Mi Hair' by Jeff Unsworth. Reproduced with kind permission.
p53 'Keef's Car' from www.travian.co.uk

The publishers would like to thank the following for permission to reproduce pictures in these pages:

p6 imagebroker/Alamy; p8 Creatista/Shutterstock.com; p9 Andresr/Shutterstock.com; p11 Gaertner/Alamy; p12 Miroslav Kis/Alamy; p14 Andrew Fox/Alamy; p16(l) nakamasa/Shutterstock.com; p16(r) Andrew Rubtsov/Alamy; p17(t) INSAGO/Shutterstock.com; p17(b) INSAGO/Shutterstock.com; p20 Scott Beaver/iStockphoto.com; p21 Pierre-Yves Babelon/Shutterstock.com; p22 Finnbarr Webster/Alamy; p23 Simon Stacpoole/Rex Features; p24 CWB/Shutterstock.com; p25 Eric Isselée/iStockphoto.com; p26 Francesco Guidicini/Rex Features; p27 Stephen Coburn/Shutterstock.com; p28 Adrian Sherratt/Alamy; p29 Karnizz/Shutterstock.com; p30 20thC.Fox/Everett/Rex Features; p31 Warner Bros/TopFoto; p34 Janine Wiedel Photolibrary/Alamy; p35 Rex Features p36 Jeff Smith/Alamy; p37(t) Kirill P/Shutterstock.com; p37(b) Jaykayl/Shutterstock.com; p38 MBI/Alamy; p39 RichardBaker/Alamy; p40(l) Olly/Shutterstock.com; p40(tr) Lise Gagne/iStockphoto.com; p40(br) Dan Steinberg/BEI/Rex Features; p42 Bubbles Photolibrary/Alamy; p44 Joe Fox/Alamy p45 Yuri Arcurs/Shutterstock.com; p48 leolintang/Shutterstock.com; p49 Apollofoto/Shutterstock.com; p50 mangostock/Shutterstock.com; p51 Image Source/Rex Features; p52(l) highviews/Shutterstock.com; p52(r) picturepartners/Shutterstock.com; p55 Geoffrey Swaine/Rex Features; p.56 Oleksiy Maksymenko Photography/Alamy; p57 Juice Images/Alamy; p58 Steve Debenport/iStockphoto.com; p59(t) Gavin Rodgers/Rex Features; p59(b) courtesy of The Advertising Archives.

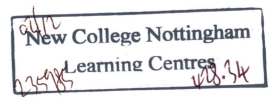

Contents

Chapter 1

AF1 Talking to others

Talk in purposeful and imaginative ways to explore ideas and feelings, adapting and varying structure and vocabulary according to purpose, listeners, and content

This chapter is going to show you how to

- Add relevant, useful details to your talk
- Add relevant, interesting details to your talk
- Structure your talk logically
- Plan how your talk will begin and end
- Vary vocabulary and sentences
- Use your face, hands and arms to help your listener understand your talk.

What's it all about?

Bringing your talk to life; structuring your talk so it is easy to follow; keeping your listener interested.

Details can be ideas, facts or opinions. If the details are **relevant**, it means they are to do with the subject you are talking about.

Getting you thinking

When you talk to people, you may give them information. Sometimes this can be pretty basic – but sometimes extra details will be useful to the listener.

Look at this example:

There has been a fight between two students at break. The Head of Year has asked a student witness to report what happened.

Head of Year: How did this fight start?

Student: Robert had been annoying Gary for a while. During break today, Robert was talking to him. Gary suddenly pushed Robert over. Then they started fighting.

- The Head of Year needs extra useful details, to decide who was really to blame. With a partner, think of two questions the Head of Year might ask to find out more.

How does it work?

The witness might add details like these:

- Robert had been picking on Gary for about three weeks.
- He often called Gary nasty names.
- Gary never said anything back.

These are **relevant**, because they are all to do with how the fight came about. They are **useful**, because they suggest that Robert started the trouble.

Now you try it

The student makes a list of extra details to tell the Head of Year.

- Robert always has a packed lunch.
- Robert said rude things about Gary's mum so Gary pushed him over.
- Gary always wears correct uniform.
- As Robert fell, Gary sort of jumped on him.
- Robert didn't have his school bag with him.
- They were punching each other quite hard.

○ In pairs, talk about each detail and decide whether it is useful and relevant. Can you explain how each detail helps (or does not)?

Development activity APP

Two students have been found damaging other students' bikes. Oliver claims he was bullied into it by Stuart. You saw them going to the bike sheds at the time the damage was done.

Is Oliver telling the truth? To help the Head of Year decide, you need to give useful details. For example, you may have noticed Stuart leading Oliver into bad habits for some time.

1 Work in pairs.
- Think of a question the Head of Year might ask.
- Jot down details to answer the question.

2 Then join with another pair and give your witness account. One of you is the Head of Year and one the witness.

Try not to read your notes. If you do forget a detail, your partner can ask you that question and you'll have your list to remind you.

The other pair will give you feedback.

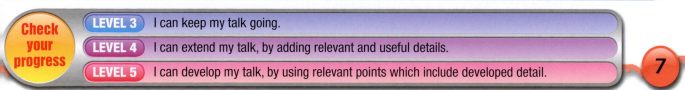

Check your progress

LEVEL 3	I can keep my talk going.
LEVEL 4	I can extend my talk, by adding relevant and useful details.
LEVEL 5	I can develop my talk, by using relevant points which include developed detail.

This lesson will
- help you to add interesting details to a simple account
- help you to make notes.

Extra details can add **interest** to the subject you are talking about – but remember, they still need to be relevant.

Getting you thinking

Luke has a new computer game called *Haunted Manor, Lord of Mirrors*. He likes it and is keen to talk to the rest of his class about it.

To remind himself what he wants to say, he jots down some details:

- You load it up and type your name in.
- You go into a strange house and find objects.
- If you don't collect all the objects you'll never get out.
- You get helpful hints along the way.

- Luke's notes only tell listeners how to play the game. Is there anything else he could mention to make the game seem more interesting?

  For example:

- Only one player at a time, but you could have a competition to see who's quickest.
- Graphics are realistic and make the place look spooky.
- Music and sounds make it really creepy.

Luke now puts each detail on a separate piece of paper. He doesn't need full sentences, just the key words so he can remember what to say, like this:

One player at a time. Competition – who's quickest?

Graphics – realistic – spooky

Music/sound – creepy

Now you try it

1 Choose your favourite computer game to talk about. If you prefer, choose a board game, or some other activity.

2 Take five separate pieces of paper. On each piece, write one detail about the game.

3 Show your details to a partner.

4 Your partner must suggest what sort of extra details would make the talk more interesting.

5 Swap your lists back. Add the details you agree with, each one on a new piece of paper.

> **Top tip**
>
> Using very short notes means you can look quickly at them to jog your memory. Of course, when you are talking you need to use full, detailed sentences.

Development activity **APP**

Look at your notes again.

1 Can you make any note shorter? If so, rewrite it. Use as few words as possible.

2 Practise looking at each note, then talking about it.

3 In a small group, deliver your talk. Add as much information as you can about each note. The others should tell you how interesting you made it.

Check your progress

LEVEL 3	I can keep my talk going.
LEVEL 4	I can extend my talk, by adding relevant and interesting details.
LEVEL 5	I can develop my talk, by using relevant points with extended details.

> **This lesson will**
> - help you put your ideas in a logical order
> - help you use your notes to do this.

A **logical order** means you are linking ideas together clearly so that your listener can follow what you are saying.

Getting you thinking

When we talk, we don't always have time to think about the order of the details. Sometimes, however, the order is important.

Halima has helped to organise a charity event to be held at school next Saturday. She wants to talk about it to her class mates, to encourage them to come along. To help her remember what she has to say, she has written some notes, putting each one on a separate piece of paper. She has decided to put them in this order.

1 Starts at 11am

2 On the school tennis courts

3 £1 entry fee for adults

4 50p entry fee for children and Senior Citizens

5 Free parking in the playground

6 Fun activities:
blindfold putting green
blow-a-balloon race
five-a-side football

7 Refreshments available all day

8 Fancy dress winner at 2pm

9 Finishes at 3 pm

The details are good:
- some to do with time
- some to do with money
- some about activities
- some with other useful information.

1 In groups of four, decide which details go together. First, copy out the box and try to fill it in on your own. Then talk about your choices and try to agree on the best order.

To do with	Detail numbers
Time	1 &
Money	
Activities	
Other information	

Now you try it

Remember, Halima wants to make this event sound like fun, so that more people will come along.

In groups of four, re-order the details so that you can try and make the event sound more exciting – for example, by starting with a fun activity. You need to be able to explain your choice to the rest of the class.

Development activity APP

You belong to a sports group. It has had a very successful year. As a treat, the organisers say you can choose an activity centre to visit for a day or weekend.

You have found details for an activity centre which you would like the group to visit.

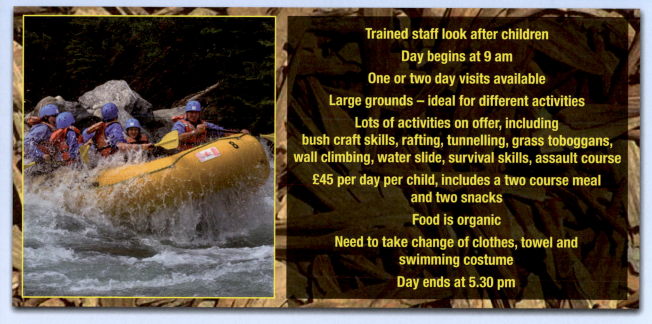

Trained staff look after children

Day begins at 9 am

One or two day visits available

Large grounds – ideal for different activities

Lots of activities on offer, including
bush craft skills, rafting, tunnelling, grass toboggans,
wall climbing, water slide, survival skills, assault course

£45 per day per child, includes a two course meal
and two snacks

Food is organic

Need to take change of clothes, towel and
swimming costume

Day ends at 5.30 pm

1 Pick 5–7 details and put each one on a small piece of paper. Number each one.

2 Add a few words to explain why you think this detail will appeal to your friends.

3 Decide on the best order.

4 Give your talk to persuade your friends to go with your idea.

Check your progress

LEVEL 3   I can organise my talk so the listener understands it.

LEVEL 4   I can organise my talk, putting things in a logical order so the listener can follow it easily.

LEVEL 5   I can structure my talk so the listener is really interested in what I am saying.

This lesson will
- help you begin and end your talk well
- help you keep your audience listening.

A good **beginning** helps to get your **audience** listening.

A good **ending** makes it clear that you haven't just run out of things to say!

Glossary

audience: the people who are listening to you

Getting you thinking

Tom is good at mountain biking and sometimes goes to trials. He's won a few prizes. His dad and brothers usually help with all the equipment but this weekend only his dad can go. He needs to get some friends to help out but they will have to work hard. How can he persuade them?

He could begin:

> I need you to help look after my bike gear this weekend.

Is that a good beginning?

Instead, he says:

> Hey! Do you want to get your faces on TV? Well, you know I'm going to a mountain bike meeting this weekend. It's not far away. My dad'll take us. Normally, my brothers look after all my gear, but they're away, so I could do with some help. The local TV news crew will probably be there, so you could be on TV.

1 Is this beginning better? Why/why not?

2 Now look at these two endings:

> I'm hoping the weather will be fine.

> Anyone interested? I'm paying for as much food and drink as you can manage!

Which ending is better? Why?

Now you try it

Your friend has asked you to go on holiday for a week with his or her family. How are you going to persuade your parents to let you go?

Of course, you need to give them some details:
- who the friend is
- where they are going
- how much it will cost.

But you need to think about the beginning and the end of what you are going to say. For example:

The **beginning**

Mum, Dad. How would you like to get rid of me for a week?

(So they'll have some peace and quiet!)

Mum, Dad. You said I deserved a huge treat for helping Granny when she was ill …

(Trying to make it hard for them to refuse)

The **ending**

When I get back, I'll wash all my clothes myself!

(Offering a deal they'll like)

I could bring you both a lovely souvenir.

(Trying to bribe them!)

When you've got your beginning and ending, try them out on two friends. Do they think your parents will let you go?

Development activity APP

Choose one of these topics:
- Going shopping
- My favourite music
- My hero
- The best sport
- The worst film I've ever seen
- The funniest thing I've ever seen

1 You have one minute to think of a good beginning and an ending that will interest your audience and get them involved.

2 In groups of four, tell each other your beginnings and endings. Who gets the most attention at the beginning and gives the best ending?

Check your progress

LEVEL 3	I can begin and end my talk so the listener knows what it is all about.
LEVEL 4	I can begin and end my talk so the audience is interested.
LEVEL 5	I can use beginnings and endings which make the audience listen and remember.

This lesson will
- help you use a wider range of words in your talk
- help you use different types of sentences in your talk.

When you talk, it is better to vary the **words** you use so that you don't repeat yourself. It's good to use different types of **sentence** too, for example long and short.

Glossary

vocabulary: the words you use

Getting you thinking

Laura is talking about 'A bad time'.

An Indie band was playing at the Club. It was Friday night. I went with my friend Julie. She said they were really good. It was raining really hard. I got really wet. That was a bad start. The Club was really crowded. I had this pair of really new shoes. They got really scuffed. Some really drunk girl was really sick over them. This really scruffy boy wanted to go out with me. The group was really bad and I have to say it was a really bad night!

1 Vocabulary:

How many times does Laura use the word 'really'?

2 Sentences:

How many short, simple sentences does she use?

Remember

A simple sentence has only one verb.

Now you try it

1 Using any word too much can make you sound boring.

Which word in the box on the right could you use instead of 'really' in these sentences?

badly	ever so	totally
very	extremely	dreadfully
mainly	brand	terribly

a The Club was **really** crowded.

b I had this pair of **really** new shoes.

c They got **really** scuffed.

d It was a **really** bad night!

e The group was **really** bad.

2 Using too many short simple sentences can also make you sound boring.

Join each pair of sentences below. You can use any of the connectives in the box on the right – but only once.

| because | so | and |
| but | which | as |

Remember

When you are talking, use as many different words – even simple ones – as you can.

Example: I went with my friend Julie, as she said they were really good.

a It was raining really hard. I got soaked.

b I had this pair of new shoes. They got really scuffed.

c The group was terrible. It was the worst night for ages!

Development activity APP

You are going to prepare a talk on the topic, 'A good day.'

1 Decide what happened on your good day.

2 Think of five things that made the day good.

3 Write a simple sentence for each one – but without using the word 'good'.

4 With a partner, practise joining the sentences together. Be as interesting as you can.

5 Give your talk.

Check your progress

LEVEL 3	I can use words and sentences so the listener understands my ideas.
LEVEL 4	I can use words and sentences to interest the listener.
LEVEL 5	I can use a wide range of words and sentence types to keep the listener interested.

6 Use your face, hands and arms to help your listener understand

This lesson will
- help you to use facial expressions to make your talk clear
- help you to use your hands and arms to make your talk clear.

Getting you thinking

When you talk, you usually change the expressions on your face, or move your hands and arms. You usually do it without thinking but it can help your audience understand what you are saying or feeling. It also stops you looking like a robot!

Facial expressions usually suggest a feeling:

Hand and arm movements can be used to indicate something:

Hey. I've got this really funny joke.

You go right to the end of this road and turn right.

Pleasure – smiling

Using an arm, and maybe pointing, to indicate direction

1 With a partner, think of facial expressions to show
- happiness
- fear
- you have had a pleasant surprise.

2 Now think of hand or arm movements that could show
- something is no good
- how thick a book is
- 'That's good. Well done!'

Now you try it

1 Choose a suitable facial expression for each of these sentences.
- 'Don't you speak to me like that!'
- 'I found my pet rabbit lying dead in its cage.'
- 'I wish he/she would ask me out.'

2 Choose a suitable hand or arm movement for each of these three sentences.
- 'What else could I do?'
- 'Your kite's stuck up that tree.'
- 'Hey! Come here quickly!'

3 Say each of the six sentences to a partner. Does your partner agree with your choices?

4 Try them again – but this time, use an unsuitable expression or gesture. What do you notice?
- Do they look silly?
- Do they confuse your partner?

Development activity APP

1 Prepare a short talk about yourself. It should last 30–60 seconds.
- Say who you are and add about five interesting details.
- What facial expressions or hand and arm movements could you use to help your listeners understand you better?

You can remind yourself with brief notes like this:

> I behave well – usually.
> (Cheeky grin, show teeth)

> Sister shorter than me.
> (Hand waist height)

2 Practise your talk with a partner. Tell each other if your expressions and hand/arm movements look suitable and natural.

Check your progress

LEVEL 3	I can use my face, hands and arms in ways that fit with my talk.
LEVEL 4	I can use facial expressions and gestures to help my audience understand my talk.
LEVEL 5	I can use facial expressions and gestures that match what I am saying.

Level Booster

LEVEL 3

- I can keep my talk going.
- I can organise my talk, with a beginning and end, to help my listener understand it.
- I can use words and sentences so my listener understands my talk.
- I can use my face, hands and arms to show what I'm saying.

LEVEL 4

- I can extend my talk, by adding relevant, useful and interesting details.
- I can use notes to help organise my talk in a logical order, with a clear beginning and end, so my listener will understand it.
- I can use a variety of words and sentences to make my talk interesting for the listener.
- I can use facial expressions and hand and arm movements, to help my listener understand what I'm saying.

LEVEL 5

- I can develop my talk by using relevant details that help explain what I mean.
- I can structure my talk, using a suitable beginning and end, to interest my listeners and support my purpose.
- I can use words and sentences that are suitable for the people listening.
- I can use facial expressions and hand and arm movements to help express feelings and ideas.

Chapter 2

AF2 Talking with others

Listen and respond to others, including in pairs and groups, shaping meanings through suggestions, comments and questions

This chapter is going to show you how to

- Listen actively to a speaker
- Make comments to contribute to a discussion
- Ask useful questions in a discussion
- Answer questions well
- Introduce new ideas
- Summarise what has been said.

What's it all about?

Taking part and listening well in discussions, interviews and general conversations.

> This lesson will
> ● help you to focus on what someone is saying
> ● help you to notice how words show how someone feels.

Active listening means paying attention and thinking about what people say. If you listen actively, you can take an active part in a conversation.

Getting you thinking

Read this script aloud with a partner. Amir is trying to tell Donna about his holiday. Jot down key words for the main things Amir wants to tell Donna.

Amir: We went to Center Parcs at Easter. It was wicked.

Donna: Yeah?

Amir: We stayed in this log cabin in the woods, with its own sauna and everything – and Sky TV. But the best thing, right, was all these activities you could do.

Donna: *(yawning)* I hate camping.

Amir: Me too – our tent leaks. But this was a log cabin.

Donna: *(looking at clock)* Do you know what's for lunch?

Amir: Oh … cottage pie, I think.

Donna: Yay – my favourite!

Amir: So, we were in this cabin …

Donna: I thought it was a tent.

Amir: A cabin. At Center Parcs. I did archery – like Robin Hood. I scored a bullseye!

Donna: I saw the film of that. It was great. What's that actor's name?

1 Try to agree with your partner about what Amir wants to tell Donna.

2 Find examples of things that Donna says and does which show that she isn't listening very well.

Now you try it

1 Ask your partner to tell you about a place they have visited. Let them do most of the talking, but listen carefully.

2 As they speak, make a note of the important points. For example:
- where it was
- who they went with
- what they did there
- when they went
- why it was special.

3 You should also
- try to picture the place in your mind
- comment now and again ('Really?', 'Sounds great' etc.) to show you are listening
- ask questions if you don't understand or if you want more details.

Development activity

We also need to work out how a speaker **feels**. We can tell from Amir's words that he is excited about his holiday. Donna only gets excited about lunch.

1 Work in a group. One student at a time talks for one minute about one of these topics:
- your ideal holiday (where, who with, what they'd do, etc.)
- something you want to be changed (a school rule, a law, a place, etc.)
- a TV programme you love or hate
- a time when you were worried (changing school, joining a team, etc.)

Speakers should try to show how they feel about their subject – for example, use interesting adjectives, perhaps stress important words.

Listeners should jot down any words or phrases that show how the speaker feels. For example: 'Dog fouling is *disgusting* …'

2 After each speaker, share the words or phrases you made a note of. Discuss what the speaker's feelings were.

> **Top tip**
>
> Speakers often stress the words that show how they feel, for example by saying them more loudly.

Check your progress

LEVEL 3	I can pick out the main points someone says.
LEVEL 4	I can follow what someone says in detail.
LEVEL 5	I can tell how someone feels by what they say and I can respond helpfully.

2 Make comments to contribute to a discussion

This lesson will
- show you how to make comments to contribute to a discussion
- show you how comments can be helpful.

In a good discussion, everyone takes part, helping to develop ideas. A helpful comment is one which moves a discussion on and shows you are listening. It can develop an idea or bring in a new one.

Getting you thinking

1 Read this conversation with a partner. Two friends are discussing what has happened to a third. Notice how both speakers make helpful comments – three of these are highlighted.

2 Find at least two other helpful comments. How do they move the discussion on?

Lucy: Hey – have you heard? Something terrible happened to Davina at the weekend.

Tania: No – what?

Lucy: Her house got burgled. Loads of stuff got nicked – telly, DVD player, her iPod.

Tania: That's awful! I'd hate that. ← *Responds sympathetically, showing understanding of why this is big news*

Lucy: Yeah – poor Davina. They broke a window and climbed in. There wasn't much other damage though.

Tania: That's something. Sometimes they smash things just for the sake of it. ← *Responds to detail. Points out that it could have been worse.*

Lucy: There was blood on the window sill so they must have cut themselves. Serves them right.

Tania: Maybe the police can do a DNA test on it. ← *Suggests how thief might be caught*

Lucy: I hope they catch someone. Davina's really upset about her iPod.

Tania: She'll probably get insurance money and buy a new one.

Lucy: Yeah, but it won't have her music on it.

Tania: She can always download it again.

Lucy: Except her PC got nicked too.

Tania: Oh, no! Still, at least they didn't get her camera.

Lucy: How do you know?

Tania: I borrowed it last term and I haven't given it back yet!

Now you try it

Continue the conversation in your own words, making comments to move it on. To help you, make some notes first, about:

- what else was stolen
- how to help Davina
- how crimes like this make the victim feel.

Development activity

With a partner, take it in turns to be A and B. If you are A, you tell B about one of the following:

- whether you think footballers get paid too much
- what you think of school dinners
- what you think are the good and bad things about your area.

If you are B, listen carefully and make comments that help to move the discussion on. Stick to the subject, but try to broaden it, like this:

> A: I think they definitely get paid too much – it's mad what they earn.
>
> B: Yes, that's true but the top players attract huge crowds and TV deals, so maybe they deserve it.

Your comments should link to what has just been said **and** take the conversation forward.

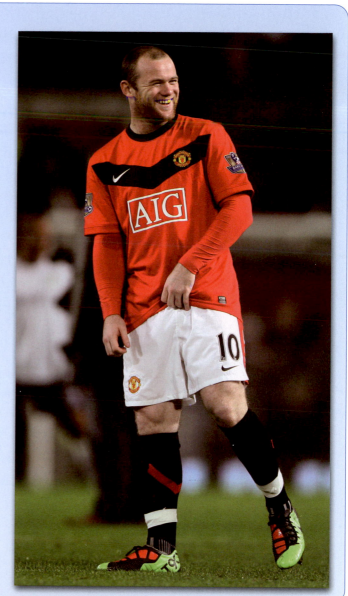

Check your progress

LEVEL 3	I can make comments that link to what has been said.
LEVEL 4	I can make comments to develop a discussion.
LEVEL 5	I can make comments that encourage others to think about a topic.

23

This lesson will
- teach you how to ask useful questions
- show you how questions can develop a discussion.

A useful question is one in which the speaker
- shows interest
- checks his or her own understanding
- asks for an explanation
- checks that the other person understands.

Questions like this can help speakers to have a good discussion, sharing and developing their ideas.

Getting you thinking

Read this conversation with a partner. Then decide how the two speakers use questions. Try to spot useful questions.

Emma: Hi, Dan. Do anything at the weekend?

Dan: We went to see my gran in London. She's not been well. How about you?

Emma: I went to see my gran too, as it happens. But she's not ill. She ran the London Marathon last week!

Dan: Wow! I don't think mine could do that. How did she do?

Emma: She came 398th, but that's not bad apparently.

Dan: Isn't it? Well, at least it's in the first 400!

Emma: Yeah – just! So, did you do anything else in London?

Dan: Yeah. Do you know the London Eye?

Emma: That big wheel thing with the glass bubbles?

Dan: That's the one. We went on that. It was cool. But my brother got vertigo.

Emma: What's that?

Dan: He can't cope with heights. He goes all wobbly.

Emma: It must be horrible. Did he take long to get over it?

Dan: Only the rest of the day …

Now you try it

Read Imran's description of his family below. Think of short questions that you could ask between his sentences. They should do one of the four things in the bullet points opposite.

> My family are quite odd. My grandfather wanted to be the first man to take a paddle steamer up the Limpopo. He was doing OK until his boat capsized. I think I probably take after him. My mother's not very adventurous. She did work for the RNLI once, but that was in an office. She does have a very strange hobby, though. My brother's a chef in a vegan restaurant. I've eaten there. The food's really good but I'd never go there again.

Development activity APP

Take turns to describe your family or friends interestingly. As you do this, ask one or two questions to check that your partner understands, like this:

A: My dad used to be a farmer until foot and mouth disease.

B: The disease that cows got a few years ago?

A: That's right. Well, my dad's cows all got it, so he went bust. He had to take a job working for the council.

When your partner describes their family, ask short questions to

- show interest
- check your understanding
- ask for explanation or more information.

Try to include at least one question that develops your partner's ideas, like this:

B: How did that affect the rest of the family?

Top tip

People usually like to be asked questions. Asking questions shows that you care about what you are being told.

Check your progress

LEVEL 3	I can ask questions to get more information.
LEVEL 4	I can ask questions that show interest and ask for more information.
LEVEL 5	I can ask questions that develop the speaker's ideas.

This lesson will
- show you how to understand questions
- show you how to answer helpfully and in detail.

To answer questions well, you need to
- listen carefully
- ask yourself what the questioner really wants to know
- think about what they would find interesting
- not just answer yes or no – give details.

Getting you thinking

Read this extract from an interview with Ellen MacArthur, famous for sailing round the world solo.

Were you always drawn to the sea? Yes, ever since I was four I've loved it. It's an amazing sense of freedom. I first got into sailing with my aunt. She had a little boat that she bought as a wreck and did up. I fell in love with the sport and the boat. The family had our holidays on the boat every summer, seven of us and the dog.

But were you secretly wishing they would all go away so you could do some long-distance solo sailing? No. I have done lots of sailing with people too.

You famously saved up your school dinner money for years to buy your first boat. What did you eat while you were at school while you were saving all the money? When I left home in the morning I'd take a banana and three slices of bread with me. Then at school I'd either have nothing or I'd have mashed potato and baked beans, which cost 8p. And gravy was totally free. I'd pile all the gravy on my plate and that's what I had.

How long did it take to save up? I started when I was eight and by the time I left school I'd bought my third boat.

1 Where does Ellen MacArthur answer a question in detail?

2 Did you spot any closed questions? Did she just answer them with 'yes' or 'no'?

3 Which question does she answer less well? How could she have given a more interesting, detailed answer?

> **Glossary**
>
> **closed questions:** questions that can easily be answered by 'yes', 'no' or another very simple answer.

Now you try it

With a partner, take turns to read out and answer the questions below. Make your answer as interesting as you can by explaining why you think this.

1 What do you see as your biggest personal strengths? (*Example: sense of humour*)

2 What things do you most value in other people? (*Example: honesty*)

3 What do you most dislike in other people? (*Example: being big-headed*)

> **Top tip**
>
> In a job interview, you have to stress your good points without actually lying!

Development activity APP

1 Write a list of interview questions you could ask someone applying for one of these jobs:
- assistant zoo keeper
- astronaut on Mission Mars
- climbing instructor
- road sweeper.

2 In pairs, take turns to ask your questions while your partner answers them. When it is your turn to answer:
- think about what the interviewer wants to find out
- try to persuade them to employ you.

Check your progress

LEVEL 3	I can listen carefully to questions.
LEVEL 4	I can answer questions in detail.
LEVEL 5	I can understand what a questioner wants to know.

> **This lesson will**
> ● help you to introduce new ideas in a group discussion.

It is important to be able to bring new ideas into a conversation. This often works better if the new ideas lead on from what has just been said.

Getting you thinking

Alex and Paul are discussing how the area where they live could be improved:

Alex: It would be good to have a cycle path by the canal. I'd use it to get to school.

Paul: Yes – and a couple of picnic places along it, with benches and tables, would be good too.

● Imagine you are a third person in this conversation. With a partner, think of other new ideas you could bring in.

How does it work?

Notice how, in the example above, Paul leads into his new idea with 'Yes – and …' Here are some other ways to lead into a new idea:

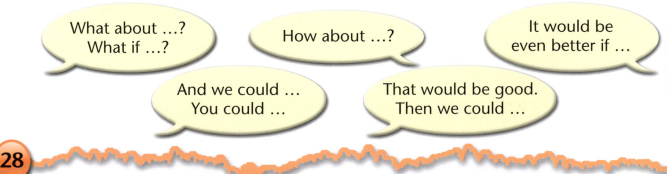

What about …?
What if …?

How about …?

It would be even better if …

And we could …
You could …

That would be good.
Then we could …

Now you try it

Now discuss your ideas for how the area where you live could be improved. For example, these could be

- things for teenagers to do
- parks and playgrounds
- shops and cafés
- cutting traffic
- stopping crime and vandalism.

Try to

- listen to others
- introduce some new ideas yourself
- use some of the phrases listed on page 28, like 'What about …?'

Development activity APP

You won't always agree with everything other people say in a discussion. Here are some phrases to introduce a new idea when you do not really agree with someone:

> All right, but …

> I see what you mean, but …

> Yes, but on the other hand …

Imagine there are plans to build a big new water park in your area. You have been asked to give the local council feedback on what it should be like.

- In a group, discuss what features you want it to have.
- When someone suggests a feature that you don't completely agree with, try to introduce an idea of your own.
- Use one of the phrases listed above.

Top tip

People will listen to you more if you show that you respect their view, even if you disagree with it.

Check your progress

LEVEL 3	I can understand a speaker's ideas.
LEVEL 4	I can show respect for other people's ideas, even when I disagree with them.
LEVEL 5	I can develop a speaker's ideas.

This lesson will
- help you to summarise what has been said.

In a group discussion, people can take on different roles. One role is the chair – this is the person who asks the questions and makes sure everyone is involved. Another role could be to summarise what has been said.

Top tip

To **summarise** is to list the main points briefly. This is helpful so that the group can see what is important in the discussion without having to remember every little detail.

Getting you thinking

1 Here is a summary of a well-known story. What has been left out?

> A girl goes into a house. She finds three bowls of porridge and eats the one that is the right temperature. Then she tries out three chairs, but breaks the one that is the right size for her. Tired, she tries out three beds, and falls asleep in the one that feels just right. Three bears who live in the house come home and find the girl asleep. She wakes up, screams, and runs home.

2 In pairs, take it in turns to tell a partner the story of *either* a book you have read *or* a film or TV drama you have watched. Use as much detail as you can.

- The person listening then summarises the story more briefly.

- The person who told the story comments on anything important they think their partner got wrong and anything important they missed out.

AVATAR

Now you try it

1 In groups, discuss what you think makes a really good film or TV drama.

Talk about

   ● your favourite *types* of film – comedy, adventure, horror, sci-fi, romance, etc.

   ● what makes a good film story – unexpected twists, tension, explosions, etc.

   ● your favourite actors and what is good about them

   ● your idea of what makes a good ending to a film.

2 When your teacher tells you to stop, one person should summarise what has been said so far. For example, you could begin, 'We all like science fiction films best, but …'

Development activity

1 In groups, discuss this opinion:

> Young people spend far too much time watching TV, DVDs and films these days.

2 When your teacher tells you, two of you should move to a new group. In these new groups, the newcomers must help each other to summarise what was said in their old group. Those who have not moved must then summarise what was said in their group.

Top tip

You can use summarising to check on your own understanding: 'Let's see if I've understood you. You say that …'

Check your progress

LEVEL 3	I can talk about what someone has just said.
LEVEL 4	I can pick out the main points and summarise what has been said.
LEVEL 5	I can summarise ideas over the course of a discussion.

Level Booster

LEVEL 3

- I can respond to a speaker's main ideas.
- I can make some relevant comments.
- I can ask questions to find out information.
- I can answer simple questions.
- I can make suggestions.
- I can take part in a discussion.

LEVEL 4

- I can listen actively to a speaker.
- I can make comments to contribute to a discussion.
- I can ask useful questions in a discussion.
- I can answer questions well.
- I can make connections and introduce new ideas.
- I can take a role in a group discussion.

LEVEL 5

- I can contribute effectively to a discussion.
- I can consider different ideas in a discussion.
- I can recognise important details in a discussion.
- I can understand implied meaning.
- I can build on the ideas of others.
- I can direct a discussion.

Chapter 3

AF3 Talking within role-play and drama

Create and sustain different roles and scenarios, adapting techniques in a range of dramatic activities to explore texts, ideas and issues

This chapter is going to show you how to

- Create a straightforward character using speech
- Use gesture and movement to show characters' feelings
- Make deliberate choices of speech, gesture and movement
- Play different roles
- Perform in different situations
- Perform in different scenarios.

What's it all about?

This chapter teaches you how to approach role-play. It focuses on how to prepare to play a character and on how to use speech and movement so that you 'become' a different person.

This lesson will

● help you explore how to create a character through speech.

How we speak tells other people a lot about us. When you are playing a character, you need to imagine how they would talk, to show how they think and feel.

Getting you thinking

Read this poem.

I'm a nooligan
don't give a toss
in our class
I'm the boss
(well, one of them)

I'm a nooligan
got a nard 'ead
step out of line
and youre dead
(well, bleedin)

I'm a nooligan
I spray me name
all over town
footballs me game
(well, watchin)

I'm a nooligan
violence is fun
gonna be a nassassin
or a nired gun
(well, a soldier)

Roger McGough

1 With a partner, decide
  ● what sort of person is speaking here
  ● how you know.

2 Read the poem to each other out loud, pretending to be the 'nooligan'. Which reading is better? Why?

How does it work?

To talk like a certain person, you have to imagine
- what their voice might sound like
- what kind of words they might use
- what age they are and what they look like, so you can start to feel and act like them
- what they think about what is happening.

What sort of person might say each of these?

> I say, old chap…

> It's doin' my head in

> All right, sport?

> It weren't like this in my day…

Top tip

They might have an accent; they might speak softly or violently; or they might sound 'posh' or croaky.

Now you try it **APP**

This time, work in a group of four.

1 Choose the character you want to play from this list:
- an old lady who is usually in charge of everything
- her feeble husband, who always agrees with her
- a religious leader whose car has just broken down
- a movie star going to a television studio for an interview
- a dustbin man, late for a dentist's appointment.

2 Make brief notes on your character about:
- where you live, your age and what you look like
- what sort of a person you are (happy/sad, married/unmarried, healthy/ill, rich/poor…)
- what sort of words you might use, for example:
  – chatty ('You OK, my dear …?')
  – posh ('Oh, my goodness …')
  – modern ('Don't diss me, man …')

3 You are all in a queue, waiting for a taxi. No taxi has appeared for 20 minutes. You begin to discuss who should have the first taxi that arrives. There are likely to be disagreements.

Remember

Great drama often has disagreements but rarely has fighting.

Check your progress

LEVEL 3	I can understand that characters speak in different ways.
LEVEL 4	I can deliberately choose how I speak to present a character.
LEVEL 5	I can begin to sustain my character through my deliberate word choices.

This lesson will
- help you develop a character by using gestures and movements that show what your character is feeling.

Playing a character does not just involve talking like them. To be realistic, you also have to act like them. For example, think about:

- how your character might walk
- their use of hand gestures
- how they use their face, perhaps raising an eyebrow or smiling.

Getting you thinking

This extract is from a story about a girl who moved to a different town.

> I shall never forget that first day in our new home. The people living around us were terrifying.
>
> As I stood at the window, I could see an old man opposite me. He looked drunk. He sat in a doorway, waving his arms around and around. Every now and then he stopped and hit the side of his head with his hand.
>
> Suddenly, he pulled himself to his feet, shaking his head. Then, frighteningly, he headed straight towards me. He had a limp and a wide smile, but his eyes opened and closed, opened and closed. As he came nearer, he pointed at me and his smile disappeared…

1 With a partner:
  - talk about **what** the man does
  - suggest **why** he might have done these things.
  - Note down as many explanations as you can for each one.

2 Then suggest what the girl probably thought about him and why.

Now you try it

Try these out on a partner:

1 Walk as if you
- are ninety years old
- have just won the lottery
- have completed your first marathon.

2 Use your hands to say
- 'I can't eat any more.'
- 'I've never been so happy.'
- 'Go away!'

3 Make your face say
- 'I hate this world!'
- 'I love you!'
- 'What is this food meant to be?'

Ask for advice, then try again.

Development activity

You have gone to the cinema.

1 Walk into the cinema and sit down.

2 Then, as you watch the film, show by using your face and hands that you find it
- confusing

then
- frightening

then
- sad

and finally
- show it has a happy ending.

3 Now repeat the actions as if you are a member of the Royal Family.

Top tip

When acting, remember your **movements** also say things about you. They can be as important as what you say.

Check your progress

LEVEL 3 I can use some gestures and movements to show how my character feels.

LEVEL 4 I can choose how I use gestures and movements to present a character's feelings.

LEVEL 5 I can begin to use deliberate gestures and movements to make my character clearer.

This lesson will
- help you focus on what to say and do when you are performing in role.

To play a character well, you need to do the right things as well as say the right things. It's not enough to just talk – you must try to actually *be* the person you are playing.

Getting you thinking

Here, a drama teacher is talking to a student who has been playing a character in a classroom play.

Mrs Phipps:	Sorry, Marek, 'No chance, loser!' just won't do. Try: 'I'm sorry, that simply won't work.'
Marek:	But, miss…
Mrs Phipps:	And as for: 'You're gonna get burned …!'
Marek:	I'n't that right?
Mrs Phipps:	No. Try: 'It will lead to serious trouble.'
Marek:	Sounds posh …
Mrs Phipps:	Exactly. Then there was 'That just sucks' and 'You can kiss my …'. Honestly!

1 What sort of a person is Marek supposed to be playing? How do you know?

2 Why is Mrs Phipps unhappy with the words he used? Who would talk like that?

3 Read the script with a friend. Sound like Marek and Mrs Phipps and show their feelings in your facial expressions.

4 Act out the script. Add gestures and movements. (Will you sit, stand, hold or shake your head?)

Glossary

facial expressions: the way we use our face to show our feelings

How does it work?

We all behave differently in different situations.

When we play a role, we need to use speech, gesture and movement to show what the character is like.

Top tip

Your level will be higher if your character seems real: use the right kind of words and make the right kind of movements for your character.

Now you try it **APP**

You have been asked to pretend you are a headteacher taking assembly. You have to speak to the school, to warn them that

- they must not go off-site at lunchtime
- anyone caught doing so will be in trouble.

You must include

- examples of recent incidents
- advice about how students should behave.

1 Make brief notes on each of these points.

2 Practise the speech.

3 Deliver the speech. You can glance at your notes for ideas, but talk to the audience, don't read!

Speak, move and use gestures like a headteacher.

This kind of behaviour will not be tolerated…

Top tip

Picture your own headteacher. How would they do it?

Development activity **APP**

There has been a fight between students outside the school grounds at lunchtime. One student's parents have been called in to school.

In a group, act out the interview, in which

- the head explains what has happened
- the parents react by *either* apologising
  or saying it is not their child's fault.

For your character, decide

- what you are like (for example, are you grumpy or easy-going?)
- how you speak
- how you might move
- what you think of the student and what has happened.

Check your progress

LEVEL 3	I can change my speech, gesture and movement to help create roles.
LEVEL 4	I can use speech, gesture and movement to help convey different roles.
LEVEL 5	I can choose speech, gesture and movement to sustain the roles I am playing.

This lesson will
● focus on ways of speaking, moving and using facial expressions in different roles.

When you are performing in role, you have to 'become' different characters. If you can do that convincingly, your level will rise.

Getting you thinking

You see this advertisement on a school notice board.

For our play, we need people for the following roles:

a professional boxer

a film star

a DJ

Auditions will be held at …

Imagine you want to audition for a part. With a partner, make notes on how you might play each role:

	How I would speak	How I would stand and move	What my facial expressions would be like
Boxer			
Film star			
DJ			

How does it work?

To play a part realistically, start by deciding what a 'typical' example of that sort of person might be like. Then try to build on that example.

If you were playing a market trader, for example, you might be loud and talk like the local people.

You might try to make your character different too.

Ladies, ladies! Get your vegetables here. I might have only one leg, but my cabbages are perfect …

Now you try it

At the audition for the school play, you are asked to pretend to be one of the characters.

Choose a character, then answer the questions below as if you were that person.

a What does the job involve?

b How long have you been doing the job?

c What's the most exciting thing that has ever happened to you at work?

d What's the worst thing that has happened to you at work?

1 First, jot down some ideas.

2 Then, in role, answer the questions for your partner. Ask them how you could improve.

3 Finally, answer the questions as if you were one of the other characters.

4 Decide, with your partner, which performance was best, and why.

Remember

Include movement and gesture as you perform, so you are more convincing.

Checklist

- Were the right words used? Which were they?
- Was there good detail in the answers? Give some examples.
- Did the movements and gestures help the performance? How?
- Did it seem like a real person speaking?

Development activity APP

1 Choose one of your characters. Imagine they are real and that they are applying to go on a game show. To see if you would be good on TV, you have to make a speech about yourself for the producer.

Improvise your character's speech.

Talk about

- where you live
- your family
- your job
- why you want to go on the show
- why they should pick you.

2 Then do a totally different speech, for your other character.

Glossary

improvise: make it up as you go along

Remember

Your characters will be very different. They will

- use different words
- make different movements and gestures
- use different facial expressions.

Check your progress

LEVEL 3	I can change my speech, gesture and movement to help create roles.
LEVEL 4	I can use speech, gesture and movement to help convey different roles.
LEVEL 5	I can choose speech, gesture and movement to sustain the roles I am playing.

This lesson will
- ask you to react differently when different things happen
- help you to choose the right words and movements to show how you feel.

If you are playing the same character but in different situations, you need to be just as believable.

Getting you thinking

Read this poem about a family being robbed.

The burglar had been and gone
and taken all we had.
My mum was shocked
and cried a lot
and was comforted by dad.

But when the burglar man was found,
he had to face the judge.
Mum hated him.
Her voice was grim.
And dad held quite a grudge.

Of course, when he was sent to jail
the family was glad.
Mum cheered and cried
(tears in her eyes)
and danced a waltz with dad.

In a group, answer the following questions.

1 What sort of things might the mum and dad say when they have just been burgled?

Add to this list:
- 'No, no, no!'
- 'This is the worst day of our lives.'

How might they sit and what might they do?
How might they react to each other?

2 Now, list some of the things they might say when the burglar has been sent to prison.
- 'Serves him right …'
- 'Fantastic!'

How might they show their happiness?

How does it work?

Everyone has good days and bad days. We behave differently when different things happen and in different situations, but we are still the same person.

If you choose the right words and movements, you can show a character's feelings. Different situations should produce different moods.

Top tip

Even when your character is in a different situation, they must be the same person – they should talk and move in the same sorts of ways. However, their **feelings** will be different.

Now you try it APP

With a partner, practise and then perform the two scenes from the poem that you discussed. Make the mum and dad seem

- upset in the first scene
- overjoyed in the second scene.

Development activity APP

Stay with your partner. Now you are playing different people. You work in a low-paid job but have saved money to go to a concert. This is a real treat. You are going with a friend.

Decide what your character is like: how old they are, whether they are lively and funny or …

Act out the following two scenes. Make sure you are the same person in each one but show how your feelings change.

1 On the way, you are both looking forward to the concert.

2 When you arrive, you find it has been cancelled. The lighting has failed. One of you is really angry. The other is disappointed, but calmer because it will take place at a later date.
   - The calm person understands why it is not happening.
   - The angry one is very upset and wants someone to blame.

Check your progress

LEVEL 3	I can adapt speech, gesture and movement to convey ideas about characters and situations.
LEVEL 4	I can make clear choices of speech, gesture and movement for characters in different situations.
LEVEL 5	I can sustain choices of speech, gesture and movement for my role in different situations.

This lesson will
- challenge you to respond, in role, to a different train of events.

As an actor, you have to show you are sensitive enough to deal with different scenarios.

Getting you thinking

A young man is looking for somewhere to stay and finds a small hotel …

He pressed the bell – and out she popped! It made him jump.

She was about 45 or 50 years old, and the moment she saw him, she gave him a warm welcoming smile.

'*Please* come in,' she said pleasantly. She stepped aside, holding the door wide open, and Billy found himself automatically starting forward into the house. […]

'I saw the notice in the window,' he said, holding himself back.

'Yes, I know.'

'I was wondering about a room.'

'It's *all* ready for you, my dear,' she said […].

'The Landlady' by Roald Dahl

1 What sort of woman is she? How do you know?

2 How does the young man react to her? What might he be thinking?

3 Is there anything unusual about what happens?

4 How might this story develop?

How does it work?

From this opening, the story could take almost any course.
However, to move it on, you need to understand

- the characters and situation
- what will happen next
- how to perform convincingly in different scenarios – for example, to make the scene frightening, sad or funny, depending on what might happen next.

Now you try it

Here are two scenarios for what might happen when the man enters the hotel:

1 The woman is utterly charming and the man has never been anywhere so wonderful.

2 The woman is weird and the hotel is the strangest place he has ever been.

Working in pairs, plan what is going to happen in each scenario.

Then, for each scenario, read the conversation on page 44 in role, like a script, and improvise the rest.

Development activity APP

You are going to give a **monologue**. Working alone, plan and practise a telephone call the man makes to his wife, explaining what happened in the hotel. You can use either scenario as the basis.

You will need to choose words and details carefully, to show your thoughts and feelings. Also, use your expression and hand movements to help show what you're thinking.

Glossary

monologue: when someone speaks without being interrupted

Check your progress

LEVEL 3	I can adapt speech, gesture and movement to convey characters in different scenarios.
LEVEL 4	I can clearly choose speech, gestures and movements to play characters in different scenarios.
LEVEL 5	I can sustain choices of speech, gesture and movement for my role in different scenarios.

Level Booster

LEVEL 3

I can use speech, gesture and movement to

- show I understand character
- show I understand what is happening
- help create roles
- help create scenarios.

LEVEL 4

I can use speech, gesture and movement to

- reveal clear ideas about characters
- reveal clear ideas about situations.

I can

- choose words, gestures and movements for a purpose
- make these choices in different roles and scenarios.

LEVEL 5

I can purposely choose words, gestures and movements to

- show precise understanding of texts and what is happening
- stay in role as the character I am playing
- develop the role I am playing
- affect the scenario in which I am performing.

Chapter 4

AF4 Talking about talk

Understand the range of spoken language, commenting on meaning and impact, and draw on this when speaking to others

This chapter is going to show you how to

- Identify and comment on what has shaped your spoken language
- Identify and comment on how we change the way we speak with different people
- Identify and comment on the regional varieties of English
- Identify and comment on how we change our talk for a particular purpose
- Explain how turn taking works in spoken language
- Understand how body language communicates what we are thinking and feeling.

What's it all about?

Exploring how and why we change the way we talk in different situations.

This lesson will
- help you to understand why different people speak in different ways.

Although we all speak English, no two people speak in exactly the same way. This is because our upbringing and experiences are always different.

Getting you thinking

With a partner, talk about:
- where you and your family grew up
- who were the important people that helped you to learn how to talk as a baby
- who helped you to develop how you spoke as a child
- who is having an influence on how you speak now.

How does it work?

From the moment we are born, we are bombarded with language from
- our family, friends and neighbours
- books, music, radios, audiobooks, TV and DVDs.

So, as we grow up, we are exposed to lots of different words, expressions and ways of talking. This influences how we talk and makes our speech unique.

Now you try it

1 Create a 'map' of who influences the way that you talk by placing four headings around your figure or name: Family, Media, School, Neighbourhood and friends.

2 Think about some of the words and expressions that you have learnt from each of these sources. Add these to your map.

Family

Expressions I learnt from my family (the word for mother, father or grandparents; terms of affection like 'love' or 'dear')

Media

Expressions I learnt from music, TV or films (words to describe different styles of music or fashion, or new words or expressions like 'spooks' or 'hip-hop')

Neighbourhood and friends

Expressions I learnt from where I grew up (names of local foods, words for things being very good or very bad, places and directions)

School

Expressions I learnt at school (the words for subjects, parts of the school day, different teachers' jobs)

3 Share your word maps with your partner.
- Were all the words familiar to you?
- Was their vocabulary fairly similar or different?

Talk about any differences you discovered.

Development activity APP

Think about your own spoken language. This is what one student wrote about the way he talks:

> I watch a lot of American TV and have picked up some of their expressions like 'duh!' It really annoys my dad!

Try to write three short statements about how you talk. You could start by saying where you come from, like this:

> I come from _____, where we always
> - say '_____' instead of 'hello'
> - call a '_____' a '_____'
> - use the expression '_____', which means '_____'.
>
> At home, we always call _____ a '_____'.

(Say whether everyone you know uses this word or just your family.)

> At school, we talk differently from at home. For example, …

(Give some examples of words you only use at school.)

Check your progress

LEVEL 3	I can identify where I learned some words and expressions.
LEVEL 4	I understand where different words and expressions I use come from.
LEVEL 5	I can explain how I use different words and expressions with different people.

Identify and comment on how we change the way we speak with different people

This lesson will

- help you to understand how we use formal and informal speech
- help you to describe different ways of speaking.

When we talk, we make choices all the time. **Who** we are talking to affects **what** we say and **how** we say it.

Getting you thinking

1 With a partner, create short role-plays for one of these situations:

  a Keziah has a boyfriend.
  - Role-play her mother telling a neighbour about it.
  - Role-play Keziah talking to her friends about it.

  b It's pouring with rain.
  - Ask your father for a lift.
  - Ask your teacher for a lift.

2 With your partner, talk about
  - **how** you changed the way you spoke in each situation
  - **why** you changed the way you spoke in each situation.

How does it work?

We talk differently to different people. With friends and family we tend to speak informally and might use:

- words like 'telly' instead of 'television' or 'TV'
- expressions like 'I ain't gonna' instead of 'I'm not going to'
- slang expressions like 'winding me up', 'no way', 'on the dole'.

We tend to avoid these expressions when we talk to people we don't know, especially adults, or when we talk to a large group of people – in a talk at school, for example.

Glossary

informal speech: the talk we use with friends and family. It often includes slang.

formal speech: the talk we use with people we don't know. Slang is always avoided.

Now you try it

Three students are preparing to speak in assembly about their fundraising for charity. Jamaal has got it right but Flora and Harry need help.

With a partner, look at the extracts and
- find the words or expressions that are too informal
- choose other words or expressions that would better suit a school assembly.

Jamaal

Our form has been raising money to buy football equipment for schoolchildren in Malawi.

It is a really good idea as boys and girls both love playing football and schools in Malawi don't have enough money for the right equipment.

Flora

My mum baked loads of cakes and stuff to raise money for footy gear. She's awesome at baking! I flog the tickets and the winner bags the cake. Mind you, it takes a lot of dosh for a net!

Harry

My mates and I play footy every Friday up the park. You have to watch out cos if you kick the ball into the flowers, old man Jenkins the gardener goes off his trolley! We all pay a quid. It goes to our charity.

Development activity APP

1 In a group of four, talk about how you could role-play the following:
   - telling your friends about a fight in town
   - covering the fight for TV news.

   How would you need to change the way you talk for each role-play?

2 Now divide into two pairs. Each pair chooses one of the role-play tasks to prepare and then present to the other pair.

3 After the role-plays:
   - Discuss how you changed the way you talked to make your role-plays more formal or informal.
   - Would the audience have believed these characters were real? Why/why not?

Check your progress

LEVEL 3	I can talk about some of the different ways we speak.
LEVEL 4	I can identify and comment on different ways of speaking to different people.
LEVEL 5	I can explain what effect different ways of speaking may have on the listener.

3 Identify and comment on the regional varieties of English

This lesson will
- help you to understand that we use different words and ways of speaking in different parts of the country.

Where we grow up influences how we talk.

At school and work, we tend to use **Standard English** but at home or with friends we may use a variety of English that has been shaped by where we grew up. We call this a **regional variety**.

Getting you thinking

- Which of these foods have you heard of: bangers and mash, laver bread, jellied eels, biryani, stottie cake, Yorkshire pudding?
- If you were having a sandwich, would you have a bun, roll, naan, sarnie, buttie, barmcake or …?
- What local words or expressions do you use? For example, for 'friend' do you say 'mate'?

How does it work?

Everyone may know the word 'sandwich' but each region has its own local words for it too.

Words may also be **pronounced** differently, so our **accent** can give a clue about where we grew up.

Now you try it

1 With a partner, take turns reading one line from each of the two versions of the poem 'Washing my hair'.

2 When you are both clear about what is being said, talk about:
  - what word people in Lancashire might use instead of 'dirt'?
  - how the poet says people in Lancashire pronounce 'falling' and 'getting'?

Lancashire: Waash'in mi hair

Think al wash mi hair ter neet.
It's gerr'in full er dir't.
It's full er muck un dandruff.
It's faw'in on mi shirt.

Standard English: Washing my hair

I think I'll wash my hair tonight.
It's getting full of dirt.
It's full of dirt and dandruff.
It's falling on my shirt.

3 Take turns reading the two versions of 'Keith's car', then talk about the following.

- In Essex, which letters are not pronounced in words like:
  - 'have' and 'his'
  - 'motor' and 'blighter'?
- In Essex, 'th' is pronounced as 'v' in words like 'with', or 'f' in words like 'think'. Can you spot an example in 'Keef's car'?

Essex: Keef's car

"The pleece 'ave called our Keef again
Some bligh'ers pinched 'is mo'er.
A villain's gorn an' crunched it up."
"Cor blimey wot a joker!"

Standard English: Keith's car

"The police have phoned Keith again.
Some awful person has stolen his car.
A criminal has crashed it."
"Good grief what a terrible man!"

Development activity APP

1 Talk to your partner about how people speak where you come from.

- Do they drop 'g' at the end of words like 'washing'?
- Do they drop 'h' at the beginning of words like 'have'?
- Do they use short or long /a/ sounds in words like 'dance'?
- Do they use different words for some things?

2 Write a short paragraph on each of the following.

- What my local accent sounds like:

  In _____, we pronounce things differently from Standard English. We ...

- What local words are used:

  We have some interesting words, such as '_____' which means '_____'

- What people from other parts of the country think about the way I speak:

  When I say some words like _____, people from other parts of the country think...

Check your progress

LEVEL 3	I can talk about my own regional accent and use of local vocabulary.
LEVEL 4	I understand how accent and vocabulary may be different in different parts of the UK.
LEVEL 5	I can explain what effect using a regional accent or SE may have on the listener.

4 Identify and comment on how we change our talk for a particular purpose

This lesson will
- identify how we talk when giving instructions
- comment on how presenters give instructions on TV.

As you know from your work on reading non-fiction texts, we talk in different ways for different purposes, for example to
- give instructions
- give directions
- persuade someone
- argue
- explain how something works or how something happened.

Getting you thinking

With a partner, take turns to be a TV chef. Give instructions to the viewers (your partner) on how to make popcorn, pizza, a cup of tea or your favourite snack. You'll need to mime or imagine the food and equipment!

How does it work?

When we give someone instructions (in this case, about making some food), we
- say what we are making at the start
- give clear step-by-step instructions, using words like 'first', 'then', 'after that', 'finally'
- use verbs to start some sentences, like 'cut', 'chop', 'mix', 'spread'.

When we are giving spoken instructions, we also
- **look** directly at the camera/audience
- **show** people step by step what we are doing or making.

Now you try it

1 Your teacher will show you a clip from a cookery programme. Each group in your class should listen and watch for different things:

Group 1	Group 2
When do they tell us what they are making: at the beginning, middle or end?	Jot down verbs like 'cut', 'chop', 'mix', 'beat' when they are used to start a sentence.
Group 3	**Group 4**
Do the chefs talk directly to the camera all, most or some of the time?	How often do the chefs show us what they are making? (Count!)

2 In your groups, discuss what you discovered and then choose a spokesperson to feed back to the class.

3 Copy out this table and then tick the things the chefs got right. This will help you decide whether you thought they gave good instructions!

Task: Giving instructions	✓ ✗
Said what they were going to make	
Gave step-by-step instructions	
Started lots of sentences with verbs (cut, take, mix)	
Looked directly at the camera	
Talked directly to the viewer	
Showed each stage	

Development activity APP

1 Tell your partner what you have learnt about giving instructions today.

2 Then show your skills in action by role-playing a *Blue Peter* presenter giving instructions for one of the following:
- making a paper airplane
- changing the ring tone on your phone
- washing the dog
- your choice.

Your partner will assess your role-play using the table above and then tell you how convincing you were as a TV presenter and what they thought of your way of speaking.

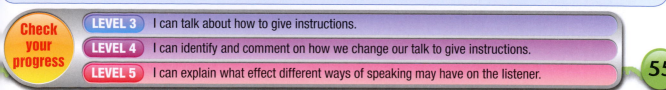

Check your progress

LEVEL 3	I can talk about how to give instructions.
LEVEL 4	I can identify and comment on how we change our talk to give instructions.
LEVEL 5	I can explain what effect different ways of speaking may have on the listener.

This lesson will
● help you to understand 'turn taking' in talk
● help you to explain how speakers know when it is their turn to talk.

When we learn to talk, we learn the unwritten 'rules' of language. For example, we learn that speakers need to take turns in speaking and listening. If we all speak at once, no one hears anything clearly.

Getting you thinking

With a partner, talk about the features of your mobile phone or other electronic gadget. Which phone or gadget would you like to own next?

Then talk about:
● who spoke first
● how you knew when it was your turn to talk.

How does it work?

We listen for 'clues' to let us know when it is our turn to talk. We listen to **how** things are said, so that we know when someone has finished:

● **Statements:** our voice often goes **down** at the end.
● **Yes/no questions:** our voice tends to go **up** at the end of these.
● **Pauses:** we tend to leave a **little gap** between one person's speech and the next, so a pause might mean that it's our turn!

Glossary

yes/no questions: questions that can only be answered with a 'yes' or 'no'!

Now you try it

1 With a partner, practise acting out the scene on the next page.

Adam (A) has gone to get his hair cut at a local salon. B is the hairdresser.

A: Hi. I'm here for a haircut.

B: Do you have an appointment? … We're pretty full today.

A: Yeah, yeah … 1.30.

B: Adam, right?

A: *(nods)*

B: Can you come through? (**A** *follows* **B** *into salon*) Have you been here before? *(drapes cape around shoulders)*

A: Nah, my Mum comes here though.

B: Oh yeah? Right. So what are you having done today?

A: Well … like … I want it cut like in this picture. *(shows picture)*

B: Wicked … and the sides shaved?

A: Shaved … er …

B: Will Mum be OK with that?

A: Yeah … nah … no probably not, so just a number 3.

B: *(nods)* OK. So … where are you going on holiday this year?

2 Join another pair and take turns at being **performers** and **observers**:

- The performers should make their speech natural and realistic.
- The observers listen carefully, identify which of the turn-taking 'clues' the performers are using and give some feedback.

Development activity APP

Your teacher will show you a clip from a TV programme called *The Clangers*. The characters don't speak English but their rules for taking turns, asking questions and making statements are clear.

1 Listen carefully and, with a partner, try to work out what their rules are. How could you tell when questions were asked and statements were made?

Did they use any other feature?

2 Are the Clangers' rules similar to ours? Write a short paragraph explaining how we let listeners know it is their turn to talk.

Check your progress

LEVEL 3	I understand what is meant by 'turn taking' in spoken English.
LEVEL 4	I can identify some turn-taking techniques in spoken English.
LEVEL 5	I can explain how speakers know when it is their turn to talk.

This lesson will
- identify how body language is used to show feelings
- understand how body language changes with different people and in different places.

Body language is the term we use to describe how we communicate our thoughts and feelings through our movement.

Getting you thinking

How good are you at reading body language? In pairs, take turns to mime how you feel when you are waiting for:

- a bus
- a present to arrive
- a girlfriend or boyfriend to phone
- exam results.

Your partner must guess how you are feeling, for example nervous, excited, worried or bored!

How does it work?

Body language can tell us about how people feel without any words being spoken and without them realising it!

It includes:

Eye contact: looking into someone's eyes or looking away

Gesture: moving your hands

Facial expressions: smiling, frowning, scowling

Movement: moving your legs, your arms or even your whole body.

Now you try it

1 Talk to your partner about this picture. Decide how the teenager is feeling. Think about
   - the look on her face
   - where she is looking
   - the way she is sitting.

   If you could read her mind, what would you write in the thought bubble to show how she is feeling?

2 Look at the body language of these men.

The referee is holding a card in the air. What does this gesture mean? Why do you think he is holding the card up like this?

What does the body language of the player on the left tell us?

3 Look at the body language of the couple in *Slumdog Millionaire*. The girl and the boy are standing very close together. What does this suggest about their relationship?

Who do you allow to stand as close as this?

Does **where** you are affect how close you will let other people be to you?

Talk to your partner about how close you can stand in

- a queue
- a crowd at a concert, dance or football match.

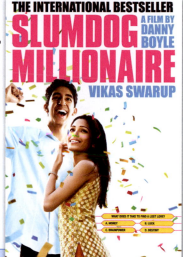

Development activity APP

When we hug someone it shows clearly how we are feeling, without speaking.

However, we don't hug everyone – and not all hugs mean the same thing!

1 Talk to your partner about when and how tightly we hug different people:
- friends
- family members
- a girlfriend or boyfriend
- another supporter at a football match.

2 What gestures do boys and men sometimes use instead of hugging?

3 Choose one or two examples of body language and write a short 'Guide for Martians' advising them
- who they can use it with
- when they should or shouldn't use it.

> **Example**
> - drumming a pencil while listening to someone speak
> - smiling all the time
> - staring into someone's eyes
> - hugging someone.

Check your progress

LEVEL 3	I can describe different body language and comment on how it shows people's thoughts.
LEVEL 4	I understand how body language changes in different situations with different people.
LEVEL 5	I can explain the effect of appropriate and inappropriate body language.

Level Booster

LEVEL 3

- I can make simple comments on how I talk.
- I can describe how I make my talk more formal or less formal with different people.
- I can talk about how I change my talk for different purposes.
- I can talk about how people take turns when talking.
- I know ways in which body language shows what we are thinking.

LEVEL 4

- I can show I understand how I talk: my accent and vocabulary.
- I can identify formal and less formal features in my talk with different people.
- I can identify some of the techniques used when talking for different purposes.
- I can identify different turn-taking techniques in talk.
- I can show I understand how body language reveals what we are thinking.

LEVEL 5

- I can explain how people talk differently in different parts of the country.
- I can explain how and why I change my talk with different people and in different situations.
- I can explain some of the techniques used when talking for different purposes.
- I can explain how speakers know when it is their turn to talk.
- I can explain the effect of body language on the listener.

Teacher Guide

Where the final task of the double-page section is substantial enough to provide a snapshot of students' progress, this has been marked as an **APP opportunity**.

Each double-page section ends with a **Check your progress** box. This offers a levelled checklist against which students can self- or peer-assess their final piece of work from the **Development** or, occasionally, **Now you try it** sections.

The end of chapter **Level Booster** is a less task-specific checklist of the skills students need to master to reach Level 3, 4 and 5. It can be used to help students see the level they are working at currently and to visualise what they need to do to make progress.

There is a range of audio and video material available to download from the Collins website, **www.collinseducation.com** (ISBN 978-0-00-743088-8). Where relevant material has been provided in this way, this symbol appears in the Teacher Notes.

As well as the video and audio material available to download from the Collins website, some Teacher Notes contain links to websites, including YouTube, for clips to demonstrate aspects of the lesson. If access to YouTube is a problem in your school, there is free software available on the internet that allows you to download clips and save them prior to the lesson.

To the Teacher

After they leave school, most students do some writing and some reading; but more of their time is spent speaking and listening. There can be no doubt that someone who speaks and listens well can cope more effectively with life. That being the case, it is surprising that there have been so few attempts to put together a scheme of work which systematically develops Speaking and Listening skills – particularly when those skills are assessed at Key Stage 3 and then become an integral part of students' courses at Key Stage 4.

The aim of these books is to fill the gap at KS3. The books are designed to support Assessment for Learning (AfL), and ensure every child knows what they need to do, how to do it, how well they are doing and how to improve their performance. One specific aim is to support APP (Assessing Pupils' Progress): the 'periodic' view of progress by teacher and student.

This can be an exciting process: the stimulus material is varied and the intention is that students will thoroughly enjoy their Speaking and Listening opportunities.

The books empower the students by identifying the essential skills at each level and allowing them to engage with situations and ideas where these skills can be meaningfully applied. Students demonstrate independently what they know and can do across the four Assessment Focuses (AFs). Activities are developed logically and teachers will be presented with clear evidence of how far students have progressed.

The series offers a wide range of opportunities to work alone and in pairs and groups, presenting, analysing, discussing and improvising. There is always close involvement with language, in its many forms, and students are encouraged to think about Speaking and Listening, rather than just doing it. The idea is that they should begin to make conscious choices, rather than 'going through the motions'.

In Chapter 4, on Assessment Focus 4, opportunities are provided to explore language variation and development across time, culture, society and technology as integral to the study of spoken language.

The progress made by Key Stage 3 students as they move through these lessons will prove enormously beneficial when they reach GCSE, when they will have to complete a range of Speaking and Listening assessments and, in some cases, undertake a Study of Spoken Language as well.

An explanation of the symbols used in the book can be found on the previous page.

Keith Brindle

Series Editor

1 Add relevant, useful details to your talk

This lesson is designed to show students that adding details to talk can help lift their performance from Level 3 'sustained speaking turns' to Level 4 'speak in extended turns'. For various reasons, students often do not think to add the extra detail that extends a talk. The spread involves individual, paired, group (or class) work.

Getting you thinking

You may choose to let the students read this out, like a role-play. You may have to coax them into realising what extra detail is required, by mentioning why the student is talking – implying purpose.

How does it work?

The main idea is for students to see that extra detail is often useful, even necessary, to a listener, who may well have to take some action based on what is said. The detail must be directly linked to the subject of the talk.

Now you try it

It is important that, when asked what they would add to the basic detail, students are not allowed to answer: nothing! If a student is struggling or likely to struggle, then paired or small group work can offer support. You may prefer groups of four here.

You could hold a short class discussion to compare results. This will help those students who may have been unsure of the relevance or usefulness of some statements. It is as important for the students to begin to realise why some details are relevant and useful – and why some are not.

Development activity

This activity should be done in pairs, then groups of four. Tell students that they can write very short sentences, or even incomplete ones.

The use of a friend as the Head of Year will hopefully give all students enough security and confidence to file the witness account.

Although there is no specific focus on using notes, the idea of listing details and using them, rather than reading a text, can be introduced. The next two spreads will focus more on making and using notes.

The others in the groups of four should try to be constructive. They will not be able to remember every detail, and may not be sure if all are appropriate. The important thing is they should briefly discuss each student's account, so that they are encouraged to recognise how details can be relevant and useful.

Summary

- Adding extra details to a talk can be useful to the listener.
- The extra details need to be relevant to the subject of the talk.

The focus here is on making the subject more interesting for the listener. The subject may, of course, be one the listener doesn't find particularly interesting, so the speaker has to suggest details that might create interest.

Getting you thinking

You may like to read through Luke's notes with the class first. No actual transcript is shown, so that students can see that an important function of the use of notes is to avoid reading a talk.

At the end, read out Luke's extended version unless there are one or two volunteers who will attempt it.

Luke's extended talk:

'I'm going to tell you about *Haunted Manor, Lord of Mirrors*. It's easy. You download it, then you type your name in. It only allows one player at a time, but you can have a competition to see who's quickest. You go into a strange house and find objects. You have to collect all the objects. If you don't, you can't escape the house. The graphics are very realistic. They make it dead spooky. The sounds are also really creepy. Some objects are difficult to find. You do get helpful hints along the way, though.'

The point is to draw a contrast between details which are essentially factual but do not convey anything of the speaker's own interest, and those which may be opinion but at least convey interest or enthusiasm.

Haunted Manor, Lord of Mirrors can be downloaded from: **http://www.bigfishgames. com/download-games/7835/haunted-manor-lord-of-mirrors/index.html**

Now you try it

Post-it notes make a good alternative to separate small pieces of paper for this activity. The sheets need to be separate. This is to emphasise the use of written notes as a guide to talk, rather than a script to be read.

Some students may ask if they can reorder their notes. Allow this, of course, but structuring of detail is dealt with in the following lesson. Keep the focus on the making of the individual notes.

There may be some discussion here, if students argue over the types of detail to add, but it is essential to ensure the focus is on improving the quality of the talk to others. The student has to realise that he/she is responsible for deciding which detail is best.

Development activity

Some students may struggle to think of a game or activity. It will be useful to have a list of alternatives to a computer game to suggest – or even some examples, if there are any available:

- Board games: *Monopoly*, Battleships, Draughts, *Shadows over Camelot*
- Card games: Top Trumps, Beggar My Neighbour, Old Maid. There are many more mentioned, with playing instructions, at: **http://www.bellaonline.com/subjects/5763. asp**
- Activities: skateboarding, fishing, football, street dancing, making models, face painting, and Warhammer-type games.

The last part of the activity may well need some input from you to make sure the listeners don't just take the easy option of saying it was 'all right'.

If time allows, or perhaps in a follow-up lesson, some students may like to try out their talk, although actually performing before the class may prove too daunting for some at this stage.

Summary
- Adding extra details to talk can make the subject more interesting for the listener.
- Using brief notes can help stop students simply reading out a script.

3 Structure your talk logically

This lesson involves individual, pair and some class work. There are two ideas here:

1 Arranging ideas in logical order

2 Putting notes in a convenient form to facilitate this.

In a way, idea 2 serves idea 1, but idea 2 is important to encourage students to keep practising talk without reading.

Getting you thinking

Read out this copy of Halima's talk:

'The charity event will start at 11 in the morning. It's on the school tennis courts. The entry fee is £1 for adults and 50 pence for children and Senior Citizens. Parking will be available in the school yard. There are lots of fun activities, like a blindfold putting green, blow-a-balloon race and a five-a-side football competition. There will be refreshments all day. The fancy dress winner will be announced at 2 o'clock. The event finishes at 3 o'clock.'

Then refer to the list of details Halima used. Explain that the order she used is not wrong but that there could be a more logical order, given she wants to encourage people to go.

Put the class into groups of four. Hopefully, the students will do the task with minimal help. If any struggle, guide them to this grouping – this order links together details about:

● Times 1 & 9
● Admission prices 3 & 4
● Interesting activities 6 & 8
● Other useful facts 7, 2, 5

The details in Halima's talk are all relevant, but the order is rather chronological. By grouping connected details together, the students should start to see that there are other ways to order details in talk. Ascertain that students have grouped details correctly and correct any that haven't. A short plenary is probably best here. Then students can move to the next section, which focuses on the grouping as a basis for reordering the talk so that it will have more impact.

Now you try it

Each group needs to agree an order and to be able to explain their choices. The groups then feed back to the class. Because the details are numbered, students have only to give the numerical order.

The results can be put on the board to allow students to compare results. If there are several groups, it would be best to have a spokesperson in each group to explain their group's choices.

If an interactive whiteboard is available, an alternative could be to let individual (or pairs of) students reorder the details, in front of the others, who could comment as they work. This is probably easier with small classes.

If necessary, suggest this order: 1, 9, 3, 4, 6, 8, 7, 2, 5. An alternative order is to have 6 and 8 first, to promote the fun aspect and leave the less exciting details to later – perhaps followed by 1, 9, 2, 7, 5, 3, 4, leaving cost till last.

Development activity

Explain to students that they need not worry about travel arrangements.

Although this would involve a follow-up lesson, some students may like to choose their own centre. There are many but here is a short selection of sites that may provide useful details:

http://www.millonthebrue.co.uk/activities.html

http://www.longridge-uk.org/youth-groups/

http://www.peterashleyactivitycentres.co.uk/activity_programme.html

It is important that students spend some time on arranging the order, even if they do not actually deliver the talk. Remind them that their aim is to get the intended audience, i.e. the other members of the sports group, to accept their choice, so the details need to be presented in as appealing a way as possible.

It may help them to work in pairs, as long as they remain aware that the decision on the order is an individual one, and any talk must be an individual one.

Summary
● Putting details on separate, numbered notes can facilitate grouping of details more coherently.
● Using notes can help put details in talks in a logical order.

4 Plan how your talk will begin and end

The main aim of this lesson is to get students to be more aware of the needs of the listener. It is important for students to realise that their talk may have good detail and be well structured, but that they must try to get the attention of the listener as soon as they begin to speak.

Getting you thinking

Two opening sentences are offered. The explanations are not offered in the Student Book, to encourage students to think for themselves and, hopefully, to get them to recognise the difference.

Using the first option, Tom would most likely get a negative response: there is no attraction for a listener unless he or she is already interested in mountain biking. The opening Tom actually uses, on the other hand, invites the listener into the talk by appealing to something he or she may well like.

This can be run in small groups, which can then report to a brief class discussion. If there is time, you could spend a couple of minutes asking students for alternative beginnings and endings.

Students need to see that for a speaker to antagonise or alienate the listener by a poor opening is counterproductive, whatever the purpose. The first approach in both the beginning and ending simply makes statements, which offer the listeners little or no involvement. The second approach not only invites the listeners into the talk, but can make them feel they have some stake in what the speaker is saying. Of course, students at this level will not be able to articulate this, but it will be useful if they can recognise the effect.

Now you try it

This exercise shows that talk needs not only to be carefully structured but also have an effective beginning and ending, whatever the context. In this case, the student wants to persuade the parents. Parents may be the most familiar adults to the student, but they are still listeners, and if the student is trying to get their agreement for something, the same considerations to their talk must be given.

Two examples of a beginning and ending are given, along with what each comment aims to achieve. You may need to explain these a little more if students don't see the aim quickly.

Development activity

The aim here is to focus on how to engage the listener quickly and end on a point that may help the listener remember what was said in a positive way.

This is a challenging activity. The following suggestions can be offered to students who are struggling.

- Going shopping
  Beginning: What a fun way to spend money. Ending: Your best buy ever.

- My favourite music
  Beginning: Give some qualities, such as good tunes or rhythm. Ending: Say how good it always makes you feel.

- My hero
  Beginning: Don't we all admire someone, even if they're not famous? Ending: Sum up the reasons why you think you'll always admire the person.

- The best sport
  Beginning: Refer to how good it makes you feel. Ending: Encourage others to get involved.

- The worst movie
  Beginning: Say you can't understand why anyone made it. Ending: Say you could have spent the time watching it on something more useful.

- The funniest thing I've ever seen
  Beginning: Say you've never laughed so much in all your life. Ending: Say it still cheers you up and makes you laugh even now.

You could encourage students to do one or more of the following:
- use rhetorical questions
- use humour
- make links to the listeners' own experience
- invite the listeners into their experience
- challenge listeners' expectations about a subject.

Summary
- Beginning a talk effectively can help to engage the audience and keep them receptive.
- Ending a talk effectively makes it sound complete and well organised.

5 Vary vocabulary and sentences

The aim here, particularly bearing in mind the level, is simply to make students aware that overusing any particular word usually makes a talk tedious. For example, instead of 'bad', they could use: 'the worst', 'horrible' or 'terrible'.

Getting you thinking

Read out the text, emphasising the monotony of the vocabulary and sentence type.

In order to encourage listening, and develop awareness of what talk sounds like, do not allow students at this stage to have their books open. Either in pairs or individually they should count the number of times 'really' occurs (11). Who got them all? They can then go back to the printed text to check.

The sentence activity will be too difficult if the text is heard in one piece. One option is a class activity: read out each sentence and ask whether it is short and simple. Each student can keep a tally of how many there are.

A second option is to let students work in pairs or small groups, each reading a sentence in turn, and deciding as a group. A short class plenary would clarify the correct number.

The teacher will also probably need to remind the students of the difference between a simple and a compound sentence. There is no discussion of complex sentences, as this would have complicated an already demanding lesson.

It is intended that with the excessive use of 'really' and the short, simple sentences, the students will sense the tedious effect this can have on a talk this short (just 85 words).

Now you try it

In the sentence exercise, point out that it may be necessary to leave out a word from the second sentence to fit the connective.

If a student wants to swap sentences round, especially if using 'because' in the first case, accept it.

Development activity

This is a demanding exercise, and students may not even complete a talk, let alone one that is wholly successful. Emphasise to them that what is important is that they focus on the process; that they start to be aware that using a variety of vocabulary and sentence types will help to make their talk more interesting to, and easier to follow for, the listeners.

Summary

- Select a wider range of vocabulary and sentence types to interest listeners.

6 Use your face, hands and arms to help your listener understand

The aim here is to alert students to something we do automatically.

Students need to understand that the use of facial expressions and gestures can affect the way people respond to us.

Getting you thinking

It is anticipated students will provide responses along these lines:

1. • a smile
   • wide eyes, possibly open mouth
   • raised eyebrows, mouth wide open or making an O shape
2. • thumb turned down
   • thumb and first finger some way apart
   • thumb turned up

It is not necessary in this phase of the lesson to comment on the suitability of expressions or movements.

Now you try it

Of course, these are slightly artificial; context will often help determine an appropriate expression or gesture. The lack of context here is designed to let students focus on the fact that, in most cases, the audience is looking at them, not just listening to them.

Possible responses are:

1. • screwing up nose, possibly showing teeth
   • mouth closed, turned down at sides, eyes looking downwards
   • eyes looking up, tightened mouth
2. • hands outstretched, palms up
   • arm, and possibly finger, pointing in an upward direction
   • lower or whole arm raised, with hand beckoning

Asking students to try using unsuitable expressions and gestures should hopefully let them see how disconcerting it can be for the audience. They need to realise that this can detract from an otherwise good talk. You might choose to develop this a little further, perhaps as a short class activity – pointing out that, for example, the second sentence said with a broad smile, would not only ruin the mood of sadness the speaker would wish to convey but could also suggest to the audience that the speaker is a callous, unfeeling brute. Although expressions and gestures are often automatic, students need to start being aware of their possible impact on an audience.

Development activity

Emphasise to students that, for this activity, they can still use hand and arm movements, even with notes in their hand.

It is not essential to show examples here but there are many clips on YouTube where people introduce themselves, usually as a part of a college project. Type 'self introduction' in the search box to see a list of what is available.

Some of the videos are technically poor or too long but three that may prove useful are:

• Joy Eastman: rather poor image quality, but short and she smiles and uses her arms and hands, even fingers. **http://www.youtube. com/watch?v=xPY65-4sdeU**

• Charlotte Gangler: The language may be difficult, but she hardly moves or changes expression. It's not too long. **http://www. youtube.com/watch?v=zS1s92SEi6U**

• Kris's CAS 100 B – He uses his arms and hands. Start at 21 seconds; stop at 1:20. **http://www. youtube.com/watch?v=zYh7IpG7f_c**

If you show the videos, draw attention to facial expressions and hand and arm movements – or the lack of them – before students embark on their own talk. It is advisable to edit the clip, if time allows, or at least choose the start and stop time.

If it is possible to video students' talks, this would give them a tangible record of their efforts and help them to see what has gone well and what can be improved.

Summary

Facial expressions and hand and arm movements can enhance talk in any context.

1 Listen actively to a speaker

The focus of this lesson is on listening in a deliberate and thoughtful way, engaging with what is said and how the speaker says it (for example in an angry or enthusiastic way), in order to respond helpfully.

Tell the class that this lesson is all about getting better at listening in a conversation or discussion, through 'active listening'. Explain that this involves listening to *what* is said and *how* it is said – content and style. It also means thinking about what is said, visualising and responding to it.

Getting you thinking

This should be done in pairs. Students should read the script twice, so that each student has a chance to read both parts. If necessary, give an example of a keyword, such as 'log cabin' – they do not need to write full sentences.

Take feedback on what Amir wants to tell Donna. Note that he does not want to tell her what's for lunch. He wants to tell her that

- he went to Center Parcs with his family
- they stayed in a log cabin with Sky TV and a sauna
- he really enjoyed the archery and did well at it.

Then take feedback on question 2. There are several signs that Donna is not listening well:

- She barely responds when he says he went to Center Parcs.
- She thinks he's been camping.
- She yawns, then looks at the clock.
- She gets excited about lunch, not Amir's news.
- She picks up the mention of Robin Hood, but only because it reminds her of something she would rather talk about.

Now you try it

This is a paired activity. Students could describe a place they regularly visit, or one they have only been to once or twice.

You could give some examples of possible places and details to match the bullet points. You could also give students a short practice session in

picturing what they are told – perhaps even getting them to close their eyes while you describe a scene.

Point out that making brief comments and asking relevant questions can be helpful for both speaker and listener, encouraging the speaker and helping the listener to stay focused and understand what is said. In the script, Donna never does this. You could spend some time discussing ways in which Donna could have responded more helpfully.

At the end of this activity, take class feedback on

- what students found difficult in the listening tasks
- what input from a partner they found helpful.

Development activity

The activity focuses on how content is presented, and how this reveals the speaker's feelings or attitude about the content.

If you think the group will be able to handle it, you could ask them to make simple notes on how the speaker speaks, for example excitedly or disapprovingly. A simple way to do this would be for them to underline the key words in their notes that reveal feeling, and to add a tick for positive feeling and a cross for negative.

The activity is ideally done in groups of four, though it could be adapted to pairs or larger groups. If possible, each person in the group should take on a different option, so that all four are covered. The important thing is for them to have a range of feelings/attitudes on which to comment.

It will help to keep this activity moving if you keep track of time and tell students when each one-minute period is up.

Summary

- It is important to listen well in order to take point in a discussion.
- Listening involves noticing *what* people say and *how* they say it.

2 Make comments to contribute to a discussion

This lesson aims to show that making comments in a discussion can be an effective part of listening, by explaining that comments can be helpful in establishing a link with a speaker and moving a discussion on to a different aspect of a subject. They also show that the speaker is listening, providing they really do connect to what is being said.

Explain what 'moving a discussion on' means and why it is important.

Getting you thinking

Tell the class to read the dialogue in pairs, and then pick a pair to read it out to the class. Draw their attention to the boxes. Point out that the 'sympathetic response' is helpful because it links the two speakers; they both care about their friend.

Note that it's Lucy's news, so the comments at first come mostly from Tania. Her second and third comments offer relevant information in a positive way. Lucy responds to the DNA suggestion positively but cautiously. Tania's comments about the insurance and downloading the music offer positive solutions which Lucy might relay to Davina. Lucy's comments provide a realistic balance to Tania's optimism.

Now you try it

Students imagine they are Lucy and Tania (or two boys if they prefer) and continue the dialogue. They could begin with any one of the suggested angles and move on when they have run out of things to say about it. The activity should last not longer than two or three minutes in total.

- 'What else was stolen' is an easy starting point.
- 'How to help Davina' could include inviting her round to tea, getting her to talk about how she feels, recording some music for her. Rather than just giving these options to students, you could hint at them with questions such as 'What would cheer her up?' 'What would you find helpful in her situation?'
- 'How crimes like this affect the victim' could include making them feel insecure, making them angry, giving them the problem of replacing things. Again, if help is needed, begin with 'How would you feel?'

Development activity

Students should work in pairs and choose one topic to discuss. Tell them to swap roles from A to B after two minutes. They could also attempt a second and third topic.

Take class feedback by asking students for examples of comments made by their partners that were helpful in developing the discussion. Write some on the board and ask other students to explain how these comments moved the discussion on. Ideally you will have been listening in on some dialogues and be able to cite one or two examples yourself if necessary.

Summary

- Comments help to show that you are listening.
- They can make a connection between speakers.
- They can also move a discussion on.

3 Ask useful questions in a discussion

This lesson aims to teach students how to 'shape meaning through questions', contributing to a conversation or discussion rather than just obtaining information.

Explain that asking questions in a conversation or discussion can be useful in several ways, particularly to show interest and obtain more information. At a more sophisticated level, they can be used to move a discussion on.

You could use this as an example to illustrate the point to your class:

Gemma: I love *X Factor*. It's great to see all those people who've got loads of talent but they might make it big and they might not.

Josh: What do you think makes programmes like that so popular?

Stacey: Perhaps it's that everyone secretly wants to be famous.

Getting you thinking

Ask students to read the dialogue in pairs, taking it in turns to be each speaker. Take feedback on how the questions are used:

- to show interest
- to check their own understanding
- to ask for more information
- to check that the other person will understand.

An annotated version of the dialogue follows.

Emma: Hi, Dan. Do anything at the weekend? *Shows interest*

Dan: We went to see my gran in London. She's not been well. How about you? *Shows interest*

Emma: I went to see my gran too, as it happens. But she's not ill. She ran the London Marathon last week!

Dan: Wow! I don't think mine could do that. How did she do? *Shows interest. Asks for more information*

Emma: She came 398th, but that's not bad apparently.

Dan: Isn't it? Well, at least that's in the first 400! *Shows interest*

Emma: Yeah – just! So, did you do anything else in London? *Shows interest*

Dan: Yeah. Do you know the London Eye? *Checks that the other person will understand*

Emma: That big wheel thing with the glass bubbles? *Checks her own understanding*

Dan: That's the one. We went on that. It was cool. But my brother got vertigo.

Emma: What's that? *Asks for more information*

Dan: Fear of heights. He goes all wobbly.

Emma: It must be horrible. Did he take long to recover? *Asks for more information*

Dan: Only the rest of the day.

Now you try it

This could be tackled in pairs or groups. Some possible questions are given below.

My family are quite odd. *In what way?*

My grandfather wanted to be the first man to take a paddle steamer up the Limpopo. *Where's that?*

He was doing OK until his boat capsized. *Did he survive?*

I think I probably take after him. *How?*

My mother's not very adventurous. *Was it her father who had the paddle steamer?*

She did work for the RNLI once, but that was in an office. *What's the RNLI? [Royal National Lifeboat Institution]*

She does have a very strange hobby, though. *What is it?*

My brother's a chef in a vegan restaurant. *What's 'vegan'? Is he a vegan? Why?*

I've eaten there. The food's really good but I'd never go there again. *Why not?*

Development activity

This activity could be tackled in pairs or small groups. Each person should have a chance to describe his or her family or friends. Remind students that, in this exercise, the speaker should ask one or two questions to check that their partner understands. Note that the activity also develops from the previous one in that students must ask questions to develop the main speaker's ideas, as shown.

Summary

Asking questions:
- shows interest
- can obtain further explanation or information
- can develop a discussion.

4 Answer questions well

This lesson aims to give practice in taking on the role of interviewee – or, less formally, in answering questions well in a discussion.

Start by asking the class what they think is the secret of answering questions well. Take feedback and refer them to the list at the top of the page in their books.

Explain that listening carefully involves paying attention to detail. For example, a question may have two parts. Understanding 'what the questioner really wants to know' involves only very basic reading between the lines at Level 4. Primarily, it would be helpful for students to understand the difference between an open question (one which cannot be answered very simply) and a closed question (which often invites a yes/no response). Interviewers will get better answers by asking open questions but a good interviewee, or indeed any good listener, will realise that sometimes people ask closed questions when they actually want more than yes or no. Ellen MacArthur's interviewer probably hoped for more than a yes/no answer with his second question.

Explain to students that they need to think about the purpose of the questions. In a job interview, when an employer asks, 'Why do you want this job?' they are hoping that the applicant will explain why they are enthusiastic about the job. They do not want to hear, 'I need the money'. In an interview for radio or TV, answers need to entertain the listeners or viewers.

Getting you thinking

Students could read the interview in pairs or you could stage it with two students – or both. You may want to give a little background to Ellen MacArthur. She was only 24 when she came second in the Vendée Globe solo round-the-world yacht race in 2001. This interview for the *Guardian* was carried out for its 'Small Talk' column, so is meant to be interesting in a light-hearted way.

MacArthur answers the question about school dinners in detail, and entertainingly. She actually fails to answer the final question accurately, as the interviewer asks about her first boat, and she only says that she had bought her third by the time she left school.

She shows that she understands what the question is getting at when she answers the first question. Strictly speaking, as it is a closed question (inviting a yes/no answer), she could have answered 'Yes.' However, this would have been dull and she guesses that the question really means, 'How did your love of the sea develop, and why do you love it so much?'.

The question she answers less well is 'But were you secretly wishing they would all go away so you could do some long-distance solo sailing?' The interviewer really wants to know how she came to become famous as a solo sailor, and whether this reflects her character, but she takes the question literally, and almost defensively.

Now you try it

This activity could be tackled in pairs or groups. Encourage students to answer fully, as Ellen MacArthur does for at least some of the questions she is asked.

Development activity

This activity encourages students to respond fully rather than answering yes or no, and to answer persuasively.

Students could devise their questions in groups and answer them either in groups or pairs. After a student has answered, it would be helpful for their partner or other students to give feedback on how well they answered. They could check the following:

- Did they actually answer the question?
- Did they answer interestingly and fully?
- Were they persuasive?

Persuasion is very much an example of 'content and how it is presented' (Level 4 descriptors).

Summary

To answer questions well:
- listen carefully
- ask yourself what the purpose of a question is
- ask yourself what the questioner will find helpful or interesting.

5 Introduce new ideas

This lesson aims to show students how to introduce new ideas in a way that

- leads on from what has already been said
- acknowledges the possible merit of what has been said, even if the speaker disagrees.

Presenting a new idea in a respectful way, especially one which contradicts another speaker, will encourage other speakers to keep listening open-mindedly.

Getting you thinking

Ask students why it might be important to introduce new ideas in a discussion. (If no-one does, the discussion will not develop.) Point out that introducing a new idea well means more than just changing the subject, as in:

Ali: I've got a pet rabbit.

Jermaine: Yellow's a nice colour.

Ask two students to read out the short dialogue. The task is flexible: you could tackle it with them as a class, or they could do it in pairs. If you choose the latter, take some class feedback. Point out that new ideas that clearly fit into the discussion are better.

Examples include:

- You could have a cycle path leading right out of the city.
- It could be used by joggers too.
- More children's play areas would be good.

How does it work?

Introduce the lead-in phrases. You could ask for suggestions for how they might be used in the 'Getting you thinking' discussion. (Example: It would be even better if the cycle path led right out of the city.)

Now you try it

The discussion should ideally be in groups of three or four. It might be helpful to spend a couple of minutes getting some ideas from the class on how the area where they live could be improved before they start their discussion.

Take feedback on how the discussion went. Ask what new ideas they introduced, and what phrases they used.

Development activity

Again, it might be helpful to begin with a short teacher-led class discussion on what students like in swimming pools they have been to.

Some possible features are

- flumes, with varying levels of excitement/ challenge
- diving boards
- different shapes of pool
- hot tub
- sauna
- babies' and toddlers' pool
- café
- viewing gallery.

Finally, ask the class what they have learned about introducing new ideas in a discussion.

Try to draw out of them

- why it is important (to develop the discussion, so that it 'goes somewhere')
- the fact that new ideas work better if they lead on from what has been said
- useful phrases with which to introduce new ideas, including those for disagreeing.

Summary

- Introducing new ideas moves a discussion on.
- Phrases like 'What if…?' are useful to do this.
- New ideas should ideally be linked to what has already been said.

6 Summarise what has been said

This lesson introduces the idea in the AF2 level descriptors of taking on 'straightforward roles', first in paired discussion, then in groups. It focuses on the role of summarising, which in any discussion could be a formal role (perhaps actually performed by the chair) or an informal one shared by all participants.

Getting you thinking

Read out the summary, or ask a student to do so. Check that all students recognise the story. (Those from non-UK cultures may not.) If necessary, ask what story it is (Goldilocks and the Three Bears).

Ask, 'What has been left out?' Essentially, only the less important details have been left out: her name, her knocking on the door and finding the house empty, her trying the first bowl and finding it too hot, the second too cold, Baby Bear's complaints, etc.

In activity 2, it might be helpful to give the class a 20-second warning that the first partner should be coming to the end of their story. Then tell them to switch roles, so that the listener summarises. After no more than another minute, the first listener/summariser should tell their story.

Now you try it

This activity will work best in groups of four. You will need to use your judgement and tell students when to stop discussing Topic 1 (types of film), probably after about two minutes. One person in each group should then summarise – allow no more than a minute for this. Repeat for the remaining three topics.

Take some class feedback on how easy or difficult students found it to summarise their section of the discussion. A further challenge here, should you need it, would be to ask one person from each group to summarise their whole discussion very briefly.

Development activity

This activity takes a controversial topic that all students should be able to relate to. They are free to put forward ideas for or against the proposition. For example, this might be a lack of exercise resulting from too much viewing, or TV/film being entertaining, educational and a shared experience.

You will need to tell students when to regroup. If necessary, say which students have to move, and where to. Refocus them on the task of summarising once they have settled into their new groups.

Take feedback on

- how easily the new group listening to a summary could follow what they were being told
- what similarities there were in the discussions.

Students could then help you to produce a whole-class summary of views on the subject. Put this on the board in bullet point form.

Summary

- To summarise is to list the main points in a discussion.
- This helps a group to see what is important.
- It can also help you to check your own understanding.

1 Create a straightforward character using speech

This spread is designed to make students begin to think about the sort of character they are playing and how that person would really speak, so that they can produce a convincing portrayal. It involves paired, group and individual work. Here, 'straightforward' means 'without complexity'.

Getting you thinking

Ask students to read through the poem in silence, to get an idea of what it is about. The paired discussion will focus their minds on how people speak and the way we react to their speech – encourage students to make notes to refer to later. Then conduct a class feedback session to explore why decisions have been made. For example, students might refer to

- the short lines
- the words used
- the spelling, and what that suggests about the character
- the lines in brackets, and what they suggest about the character.

Hopefully, when they read the poem out loud, students will now adopt a speech style different from their own. You might suggest they adopt an accent, speak more loudly or more slowly, for example. The idea is that they should enjoy the reading.

Encourage some students to perform for the rest of the group. How many different-sounding 'nooligans' has the class produced? You might discuss why they decided to say particular words and lines in the way they did and what sort of person they guess is speaking. The more convincing ones might have spoken more clearly or tried to use an accent.

'Stereotyping' is likely to be a key consideration throughout this lesson. When it crops up, discuss how we are all tempted to stereotype, but need to recognise that everyone is actually an individual with their own interests, fears, loves, history …

How does it work?

This offers the opportunity for a brief class discussion about how you can't just 'be' a person: if you want to convince an audience that your character is real, you have to know things about them. Ask students if they have come across people (real or in the media) who have speech characteristics that make them different. You could also discuss how we judge people on the basis of how they look, how they move and, crucially here, how they speak.

Using the examples as a starting point, you could ask what words their grandparents use that they don't, and vice versa; have they spotted newsreaders using particular words and phrases; and so on.

Now you try it

Moving into groups of four, students select from the list of characters offered. You could add to their options but too many alternatives will result in a longer selection process and delay the next stage.

Instead of just reading the lines of the 'nooligan', students now develop some speech of their own, appropriate for their character in the situation offered. The idea of the background notes is to make their offering more substantive, though at this level they are still likely to be dealing in stereotypes. The important point is that they should be aiming to perform as someone very different from themselves.

With regard to the words used, discuss how different people might express their displeasure – what an American might say, for example, ('Gee, that sucks, man') or the Queen ('One is simply not amused').

Students might never have been in a taxi queue – if that is likely to be a problem, the setting could be a queue for train tickets when the ticket machine has broken, for lunch when the till has broken, or anything appropriate. Whatever you decide upon, it is necessary for there to be an argument, so it can lead into the development activity.

Ask some groups to perform for the class, briefly discussing the characterisations, what we think about the characters involved and why. Point out any good examples of speech that suggest character.

If appropriate, students could tackle the following extension activity:

The argument at the taxi rank became very loud. The police were called. Everyone was arrested for disturbing the peace.

Stay in role as the same character. In court, the judge asks you to explain what happened, in your own words. Tell the judge what happened.

The judge's role should **only** be to ask what happened. The idea is that they can talk at greater length (in the argument, their input might well have been brief). The better ones might even sustain the character, which is moving them towards Level 5.

Summary

- We judge people in part by what they say and how they say it.
- To portray a character convincingly, we need to use our imagination to 'enter into' their way of life, attitudes and speech patterns.

2 Use gesture and movement to show characters' feelings

This spread encourages students to act more convincingly. It also stresses the need to use their bodies, hands and faces to make a character more convincing, showing the character's feelings. Again, 'straightforward' means 'without complexity'. Although the first section requires students to work together, elsewhere they are developing their own responses and can be supported by friends or classmates.

Getting you thinking

The extract can be read by the students in their pairs, or be read out to them. This might be preferable if the content might worry any of them!

When answering the questions, they should be encouraged to offer alternative interpretations for the man's actions, working through each one in turn. It will probably be best to get them to write their answers. Encourage them to be imaginative in their explanations.

Answers should be discussed with the class. The 'why' of question 2 can open a discussion of how we judge people – often instantly – and respond to how they look and behave.

Students can also act out their own interpretation of the scenario, perhaps using thought tracking – speaking her thoughts aloud – to explore what the girl was thinking about the man, and why.

Now you try it

Although the activity is intended to provide some humour, it is vital that students get the idea that performances can be improved and polished. Stress that partners should be honest in their assessments and offer clear guidance for improvement. If a performance is not totally convincing, it needs to improve.

You might stop the class to highlight one or two students in rehearsal, and discuss their qualities

at that point. This will emphasise that these things need to be 'worked at'. Sitting three or four students side by side in front of the class to perform reveals the different ways the meanings can be registered and can be an effective comparative exercise.

For each activity, watch some performances and discuss with the group why they are good and how they might be improved. Deliberately choosing and reflecting on gestures and movements is key to achieving Level 4.

Development activity

Activity 1 can be done in pairs, though it will provide a good class exercise. Seat a number of students facing the rest of the class. Then say that the film has become 'confusing'; then it is 'frightening' (possibly, then, 'even more frightening'); and so on. The audience can judge how well the performers have done. It is likely that 'over-acting' provokes the most laughs and is regarded most highly, but give credit to quiet but realistic offerings.

Activity 3 will need rehearsal, but can be done in small groups, with the students taking turns to perform. They can then discuss qualities and continue, with the imperative that the next performance should try to improve on what has gone before.

Summary

The students should be aware of

- how to use gesture, expression and movement to reveal characteristics and feelings
- the fact that we judge people, in part, by what we see of them.

3 Make deliberate choices of speech, gesture and movement

This lesson brings together and reinforces the skills dealt with in the previous two, trying to encourage a range of techniques when students perform. It incorporates attempts to move them away from just speaking in role, so that they also begin to move and feel like the person they are portraying. The initial paired work lets them work out ideas together; 'Now you try it' allows them to focus their attention individually on the new concepts; and the Development activity demands that they use speech, gesture and movement when working with others.

Getting you thinking

The initial script could be introduced to the whole class at once, with students reading, or could be dealt with from the start in pairs. You might like to discuss whether this is typical of a drama lesson, where the class's sympathies lie, etc.

Students then work on the questions in pairs. Discuss the answers they produce. You might wish to interrupt some pairs whilst they are working on number 3 and ask the class for comments. See if any pair is changing the expressions sensibly with each line. Ask the class why this is particularly impressive.

Watch some of the final performances and focus attention on instances where words, gestures and movements are effectively combined.

Now you try it

To make a convincing speech, students will probably have to make notes. It will certainly be helpful if they know how to use sub-headings and bulleted points, because it must be emphasised that they must not read. For some, it might be necessary to let them use the notes for initial practices, then have them speak without any notes at all. The speeches are likely to be quite brief; however, it is the quality of performance that is the key here.

You might want to offer some advice on the sorts of things headteachers say, for example: 'We should have respect for each other'; 'Bad behaviour will not be accepted'; 'School rules are important'. Also, it might be that the head moves around a stage, pausing to make the important points – or stands very still, looking threatening…

Stress

- the way in which the headteacher's face is likely to support what is being said (possibly demonstrating this)
- the fact that the headteacher can make arm gestures or hand gestures.

Watch some performances and allow the class to comment. Again, draw their attention to the fact that speech, gesture and movement are really effective if used together and convincingly. If time permits, allow them to improve what they have previously done, in the light of what has been said.

Development activity

Groups of three will be ideal for this. When they have decided which parts they are playing, they will need a few minutes to decide what they are like, their attitudes and so on. The group will have to decide what the student has done wrong and each person will need to decide what they think about the incident. They will need time to practise.

Students could aim for a performance lasting three or four minutes. Stress that they are not allowed to fight!

Again, watch some performances, and ask the class to comment on the performers' abilities to speak, look and move convincingly, rather than on what the student is supposed to have done or on the rights and wrongs of the situation.

Ask the class to comment on what impression they had of each character. Was it what the student playing the character had intended?

Summary

Speech, gesture and movement all need to be used to be convincing in role.

4 Play different roles

This lesson stresses the need to imagine 'background' in order to play characters convincingly, then allows students to focus on two very different characters. After working out what their characters are like, they first answer a series of questions in role, then make a longer speech as each of the characters, to encourage them to extend ideas and, if possible, sustain the performance.

Getting you thinking

Obviously, different 'types' could be chosen for them to make notes on (a holiday rep, a police officer, and so on) but the important thing is that they should be very different from each other. Make sure they are working on characters they know about.

The note-making need not be extensive, but is intended to make students think precisely about what their character is like, before they begin the portrayal. There is no reason why they should not have the same notes: what they actually say will obviously be different. They might produce something like:

> DJ: I'd speak fast, using street language and modern words; I'd keep moving as if my iPod was playing music and I'd talk with my hands; my face would be calm and my eyes half closed as I nod my head to the music…

How does it work?

This section gives you an opportunity to collect ideas from the class about what a stereotypical boxer might be like, etc. Possibly allow some students to demonstrate a walk, or how they might behave if they saw a rival fighter, and so on.

Now you try it

After the preparation, the students will, logically, work in pairs. Groups could be used, of course, to give a wider range of comment. Make sure you allow time for some performances to be shown to the class and commented upon. One key element will be the content, but also have students pay attention to how the character 'comes across': are the students who perform giving a realistic representation of the character, or merely saying the right things?

Development activity

After some preparation, this allows them to speak at greater length and demonstrate their ability to speak, move and gesture in an extended situation. The two performances from each student should be very different.

If time permits, this would be an excellent opportunity to video some of the students so that discussion of their qualities can be more informed and individuals can be encouraged to see exactly what they themselves did well and decide which sections might have been improved, and how.

Summary

Ask students to reflect on the difficulties they might have found in playing different roles, but try to move them to an understanding of the fact that portrayals are always more convincing if you have some background for your character, and if you try to function exactly as that character would in real life. A willingness to move from who you are into the mind and body of a different person makes the acting easier.

Students should be encouraged to observe closely how people talk and move in real life, as well as watching how actors create realistic performances.

5 Perform in different situations

The emphasis in this lesson is on students maintaining a character but responding differently in different situations. After an initial discussion about how two adults react to a harrowing event, there is an opportunity to perform the roles but at different stages in the story. There is an extension exercise in which the students begin with the same emotions but then respond in different ways to what happens.

Getting you thinking

The questions can be answered in pairs or small groups, ideally with one member taking notes to feed back to the rest of the class at the end.

For Activity 1, ask students to produce as long a list as possible of exclamations or likely statements. For how they might sit, input ideas as necessary: they might be on the edge of chairs; they might not be able to sit still; they might get up and wander round the room …

With each other, pointing, they might be blaming each other for what has happened ('You didn't lock the door…'), or they could be comforting each other…

For Activity 3, again ask for detail. Their happiness will be relayed in what they say and in the details from the poem, but they might also sit in total happiness or kiss …

How does it work?

Talk with the class about how people behave differently in different situations. Stress, however, that when acting in different situations the same character should still be recognisable. You might suggest that a character with a limp will still have it, that a character with an accent will maintain it, and so on. However, emotions change, so the challenge here is to be credible as the same person but able to register different feelings, stemming from what has happened.

Now you try it

The students will have to make essential decisions before beginning, but this must be done quickly:

- What are the parents like?
- How has the burglary taken place?
- What has been stolen?
- How long is it between the robbery and the trial?

- What has happened to the family in the meantime? (Did they have insurance? Have they had to buy everything new? Has their life been 'destroyed'?)
- Do we know anything about the burglar?
- What celebrations might they have at the end?

Depending on the nature of the group, this might be a useful opportunity to pick out a few techniques they could use, for example:

- a silent section as they gaze at their house after the burglary, so we feel their dismay and sense of loss
- a character talking out into the audience, in a short monologue, to show feelings
- freezing the action right at the end, so that how the characters feel is left in a freeze frame for the audience.

Obviously, the middle stanza of the poem has not been used here: a third scene can be added, if time permits.

Allow students to comment on performances and 're-draft' them if possible, taking on board the criticisms.

Development activity

It is vital that the students decide who they are and what sort of person they are (age, background, etc.) before they start. They can choose their occupation, but 'low-paid' has been specified to make the outing seem very special.

The planning period will also require them to decide who they are going to see, where the first scene will take place (on a bus?) and how they hear about the postponement. Stress that their emotions are likely to be similar in the first scene, but very different in the second. They must, though, be recognisably the same character (so they might have the same phrase they use regularly and might mention the same incidents, for example).

You can stop practices at various stages, to highlight performances as they develop, and view some completed scenes, for comment, at the end.

Summary

The lesson has been intended to encourage students to respond appropriately in different situations, whilst maintaining a character. If they have adapted and sustained the role suitably, the lesson will allow them to access Level 5 criteria.

Using a set starting point, this spread is designed to have students respond to different scenarios, demonstrating appropriate reactions. After studying the initial situation, they can attempt two different outcomes – then, in a development activity which extends the events, they work alone, reporting what has happened by phone.

Getting you thinking

This is initially a reading task, which can be undertaken alone, in pairs or groups. However, since it is the basis for what follows, a sharing of ideas will be required so that all students can move on from it.

Focus discussion on the use of language ('Out she popped', *Please*, 'pleasantly', '*all* ready', 'my dear'; 'made him jump', 'automatically starting forward', 'holding himself back') and what each word or phrase might suggest.

How does it work?

Following the discussion, students should have the knowledge required and should already have discussed possible developments. Stress now the need to make their own performances as convincing as possible. They should try to visualise the landlady and the young man, so that they can play them with conviction: How old are they? How do they walk? How do they speak?

Remind the students that these are requirements for any performance.

Now you try it

This will need planning time. You might like to collect some ideas from the class before they begin, to help others. Also, it might be better to have them work on one scenario, then review their performances before moving on to the second one.

Presumably, Scenario 1 will demand ideas of luxury or opulence, so they will need to respond to what is 'around them'. The man might well be treated like an honoured guest or long-lost relative. Scenario 2 allows them to create a weird or frightening world, which again has to be reflected in what they say and do.

Have the class comment on how well different pairs have coped with the different scenarios. You can use the 'Check your progress' box to do this:

- What level do you think this performance is and why?
- Did they deliberately choose speech, gesture and movement to convey clear ideas about characters in this scenario?
- How could they improve?

Development activity

Talking alone can be more demanding, though in this case they are reporting what has happened. More able students are likely to include emotion as they react. Before they begin to practise, show how a face or hands can still be used, even when phoning, to register feelings.

More able students should be able to imagine what is being said at the other end of the phone. There will be pauses and they can respond to unheard questions.

As usual, individual students can be highlighted as they prepare and feedback at the end is essential.

Summary

When planning any role-play, students should always consider possible developments so that they can select the most suitable scenario. However, events should always have a credible extension, so all the relevant details should be decided upon before beginning to act.

Those who can make their performances believable in different scenarios will be most successful when role-playing.

1 Identify and comment on what has shaped your spoken language

The aim of this lesson is to get students thinking and talking about how they talk and how they acquired, and continue to expand, their language. Students may be surprised to discover that their language may differ from someone else's.

Getting you thinking

As this is likely to be the first time students will have thought about what makes up their spoken language, help them to explore the influences on their language by asking questions such as:

- Who taught you your first words?
- Who did you spend a lot of your pre-school time with?
- Did someone read to you?
- Who influences you now?

You may want to have maps of the UK and the world available, so that students can show where they or their families came from or grew up.

How does it work?

Encourage students to see that language is acquired over time and is enriched by new words and new expressions throughout our lives. You could ask them to write down the words they think they learnt first and the words they've learnt most recently, to give them a sense of progression.

Students might be interested to hear about Helen Keller, who was blind and deaf from the age of two and who learned to speak through sign language. Her teacher spelled out the word 'water' on one palm while holding her other hand under a running tap. Helen said that through this experience she realised that 'everything had a name … every object (she) touched seemed to quiver with life'

Now you try it

The class can either work on one section of the 'map' at a time, or different pairs can tackle different sections. You might want to show some TV clips for the **Media** section. Let them watch a minute or two and ask them to note down 'unusual' phrases such as:

- 1970s expressions like 'Fire up the Quattro!' in *Life on Mars*

- space or sci-fi expressions from *Doctor Who*.

Alternatively, you could offer them some questions to think about. For example:

For **Family**, you could write on the board:

- relationship terms (mother/grandmother; father/grandfather) and what they call that person
- terms of endearment, such as 'honey', 'sweetie', 'lazybones'!
- what they call the meal they eat at 6 o'clock ('tea' in the North, 'dinner' in the South)
- any words or phrases for common household objects such as TV, oven or vacuum cleaner.

For **Neighbourhood and friends**, you could ask how they say:

- Go shopping – Go up/down town/street/shops (or other)
- good looking – fit?
- children – kids? bairns?

For **School**, you could ask them to jot down ten new words used in secondary school: homework, curriculum, physics, compass, etc.

Check which words and expressions they know and which are new to them.

Development activity

Students need to learn to write about their language. Allow them to rehearse their comments orally with a partner before writing.

While an exemplar sentence and some sentence starters have been given, do encourage Level 4 students to construct their own sentences commenting on the words and expressions they use and how they acquired them.

Summary

Language is acquired and words and expressions are not only learned but may vary

- in different contexts, such as home or school
- in different parts of the country
- with different people, such as friends and family or staff at school.

2 Identify and comment on how we change the way we speak with different people

This lesson is designed to get students talking about how we use formal and informal varieties of English with different people.

Getting you thinking

This activity is to encourage the groups to talk about **how** their characters should speak, not just what they will say.

Ask one or two pairs to perform their role-plays in front of the class to ensure that everyone sees the difference between speaking more formally and more informally.

How does it work?

Explain the terms formal and informal speech – the diagram below might help. Ask them to place conversations they have had today on the line and help them to see that this is a continuum rather than 'either/or'.

Formal (an interview)	→	Casual (a chat with friends)

Alternatively, you could show clips of TV programmes to show the differences. Formal and informal speech in 'interviews' can be watched in *Creature Comforts* at **http://www.youtube.com/watch?v=Ob-OVUoJ1RM**.

Point out that it is important to know **when** to use formal speech. Students could be asked to think about a situation for each of the following examples:

- meeting people for the first time
- talking to people we don't know
- public speaking, such as a wedding speech or a vote of thanks to kitchen staff after the school's Christmas lunch.

Now you try it

Either read Jamaal's extract aloud or ask a student to. Point out that it is formal and well organised. Jamaal avoids

- abbreviations and contractions
- informal vocabulary like 'kit' for equipment and 'kids' for boys and girls

Pairs can then read the remaining extracts to each other and discuss how to make them more formal. Students will need photocopies of the extracts on paper so that they can 'correct' them.

Development activity

This activity gives pupils the opportunity to demonstrate what they have learnt and to take part in some speaking and listening AfL. The tables and feedback could form part of the group's assessment for AF4.

Informal:

A: You'll never believe what I saw when I was coming home from the skate park last night!

B: Nah, what did you see?

A: I saw Dave Jenkins' brother thumping …

Informal style will allow slang, contractions, tag questions and interruptions.

Formal:

You might like to show the class an example of a news programme such as Sky News at **http://news.sky.com/skynews/video** to familiarise students with the more formal style.

The more formal style will use more complex sentence structures and more challenging vocabulary – no slang, tag questions (such as 'haven't you' added to the end of a statement) or interruptions. Only one person would speak at a time.

You may wish to supply students with an assessment grid:

How realistic was the role play?			
Performer's name:			
	Just right	Mostly right	Wrong
Formal style			
Informal style			
Vocabulary choices			

Draw the lesson to a conclusion, by asking pairs to use the role-plays to explain to one another why it is important to know that we talk differently to different people and in different contexts, and to explain to each other what they understand by formal and informal talk.

Summary

Students have had the opportunity to explore their use of formal and informal language and considered how who we are talking to *affects* our choice of language.

3 Identify and comment on the regional varieties of English

Getting you thinking

Ask students to brainstorm some of the foods that they love and to identify which are local or regional and which are national – or even international! Let them look at the list of foods in the chapter and talk about the familiar and unfamiliar and where the words/dishes come from.

Ask students about other local words or expressions to describe:

- good (cool, etc.)
- talking (chat, gossip, natter, have a word with, etc.)
- toilet (john, bog, lav, etc. – if you feel brave!).

Finally, ask students if they are also aware of different words/accents their family or friends use that are from other places (not their local area).

How does it work?

Make the link between local words and local accents. You could let the class listen to some examples of regional varieties from TV or film clips, YouTube or the outstanding British Library on-line collection of sound clips at **http://www.bl.uk/learning/langlit/sounds/**.

One way into this site might be to use the homepage and tick 'modern dialect' to find sample clips. You could choose by your local area, or the clips for Norwich, Plymouth, London (Peckham) and Northern Ireland (Lissumon) provide good contrasts.

If you wanted to take this further to explore how culture/ethnicity intersects with region, tick 'minority ethnic' and explore some of those clips with the class.

Alternatively, choosing the 'Your Voices' tab at the top of the screen will allow you to hear students from around the country reading from the Mr Men story, *Mr Tickle*.

Now you try it

The poems are light-hearted doggerel and students will no doubt be intrigued by the spelling! Discuss how poets and writers sometimes try to capture the way local people speak by using local words and different spellings to show people's accents.

Let students read and explore the texts. Encourage them to think about the differences between how they talk and how people in Lancashire and Essex talk, in terms of accent and words/expressions used.

Explore how students feel about people with particular accents. Do they react in a different way when they hear different accents?

You might choose to carry on and tackle the second verse of the poems:

Lancashire

I don't like lookin scruffy,
So while I've gett'n time.
I'll gi mi hair a reet good scrub,
Un hang it eawt on't line.

I don't like looking untidy.
So while I've got the time.
I'll give my hair a really good wash
And hang it on the line.

Essex

"'E says they pinched 'is mobile phone
'is CDs an' 'is jacket."
"Nah! Not 'is posh new levver one?
I bet that corst a packet."

"He says they stole his mobile phone
His CDs and his jacket."
"No! Not his smart new leather one?
I think that must have been expensive."

For the Lancashire dialect, there are lots of other poems, some with sound files, at **http://www.wigandialect.co.uk/Wash.htm**

Development activity

It is important for students to have the opportunity to rehearse their ideas orally before writing up a short description of a regional variety.

Students can attempt to 'translate' one verse of one of the poems from Standard English into their regional variety using:

- local words
- spelling to show how they pronounce the words.

It might be a good idea to have some local words and possible ways of spelling to support anyone who struggles.

Summary

Students have had the opportunity to explore regional accents and vocabulary, and how they differ from Standard English.

4 Identify and comment on how we change our talk for a particular purpose

This lesson is designed to get students talking about how we change our talk when giving instructions.

Getting you thinking

Ask students to role-play being a TV chef and giving instructions to one another. Give them an opportunity to evaluate one another's instructions with one 'It would be better if …' each.

How does it work?

Explain to students that spoken instructions share most of the features of written instructions – the main points are listed. Check that they understand what a verb is and explain that when giving instructions or orders we miss out the 'you' pronoun. Model two or three examples of instructions that begin with an imperative verb: 'cut', 'slice', 'chop', 'stick', 'fold', etc.

Get students to think about the difference between reading instructions and watching instructions on TV. The BBC website might be a useful resource here, as it has video clips and written instructions which could be compared. Go to: **http://www.bbc.co.uk/food/techniques**

Talk about the importance of
- eye contact in talk
- the presenter looking directly at the camera to engage the viewer
- the presenter showing each stage of the process.

Now you try it

Put the students into groups numbered one to four and explain the task to them. Each group is watching for one feature. An alternative is to play the clip four times so that each group has a try at each activity. The task is based around a specific clip taken from *The Hairy Bikers* but can easily be adapted to work with clips from other cookery programmes.

A number of options are available for accessing a suitable clip:
- At the time of going to press, the following URL will take you to *The Hairy Bikers* clip: **http://www.youtube.com/watch?v=1eaIYepXJIU**.
- Clips are also available to download via the Collins website.
- Alternatively, you could search YouTube for 'Hairy Bikers' or look at the BBC website: **www.bbc.co.uk/food/techniques**, which has additional written instructions that you might find useful. Files from YouTube can be downloaded using free online file conversion tools.

Screen the video clip of *The Hairy Bikers* or an alternate clip of your choice. After discussion and plenary, ask students to copy the table into their books and complete it. Their feedback about how people change the way they speak to give instructions could be used to assess AF4.

If you are using the Hairy Bikers clip, you might also want to discuss with students the fact that, because the clip is for TV, it is designed to be entertaining as well as instructional – hence the inclusion of humour.

Development activity

Students have a second chance at being a TV presenter. This would be a good opportunity to evaluate them for AF1.

Summary

- Students have explored one of the non-fiction reading (and writing) formats and can identify and comment on the techniques used in oral delivery.
- Further work could be undertaken by directing students to examine the techniques used for *explaining* (stages and logical order, visual aids, etc.) or *persuading* (emotive language, statistics, rhetorical devices, etc.).

5 Explain how turn taking works in spoken language

Getting you thinking

Model with a student what happens when two people keep talking at the same time: each of you should speak incessantly about your amazing Christmas dinner or summer holiday. Just 20 seconds should prove the point – we can't all talk at once; we need to take turns.

Allow the pairs a little time to both explore the first activity and to talk about how they knew it was their turn to talk. Take some feedback.

How does it work?

Reassure the class that learning about spoken language is not 'new' knowledge for them: they use their well-developed skills every day! We are simply finding a vocabulary to describe what we already know.

Remind students that usually, when we ask a question, we expect an answer, whereas a statement is used to simply share a point of view or an idea. The listener can reply or change the topic. For example:

Q: What is this?
A: It's a banana.
S: I like bananas.
S: I don't.

You could let them try out tag questions (added to the end of a statement to check information or seek agreement, for example 'are we?', 'haven't you?'), greetings, apologies, etc. Do our voices usually go up or down at the end?

Now you try it

Listening is a very important part of the Speaking and Listening curriculum. In this activity, students are going to have to listen for falling or rising tones.

You may want to model some clear tones for them:

✓ Rising tones for questions like:
  ● Do you want any more?
  ● Is that yours?
✓ Falling tones for statements and, if you think appropriate at this stage, for 'Wh-' questions:
  ● What's the answer?
  ● Who's that?

Allow the groups sufficient time to practise their scene and then, before they undertake the observation part, remind them that they are looking for those rules that we already know as speakers of English, but now need to consciously listen for.

After both pairs have presented, allow the groups a little time to discuss the turn-taking techniques they were observing. Did they notice any other types of sentences that either rose or fell at the end of someone speaking? They may, for example, have picked up on the falling intonation at the end of 'Where are you going on holiday this year?'

Choose one or two pairs to present to the class and take feedback on how the turn-taking techniques worked in the piece. Ensure that everyone is aware of and can comment on the three techniques in 'How does it work?'.

Development activity

There are lots of clips of the Clangers on the internet and all will serve the purpose of the exercise well. Without the distraction of content, students will be able to focus on how the Clangers use the same turn-taking techniques as we do for questions, tags, statements, etc.

Tell students they will need to **listen** carefully. Allow students to listen to a minute or two of the clip and then ask them to talk about what they can hear. Talk about how the content of the Clangers' speech is shared by the narrator, but we do gain something from how the Clangers talk to each other.

Replay short extracts several times so that students can hear the pauses and the rising and falling tones. Ask them:

● How do the Clangers know it's their turn to talk?
● How do the Clangers know a statement or a question is being made or asked?
● Are the Clangers' rules for turn-taking similar to ours?

Encourage them to give reasons. If they get stuck, refer them to the 'How does it work?' section.

Students will need to jot down notes as they listen. They can then share their ideas with their partner and the class. If you wish, they could write a short paragraph on how we let listeners know it is their turn to talk.

Summary

Students have explored how we use pauses, and rising or falling tones, in turn-taking.

6 Understand how body language communicates what we are thinking and feeling

In this lesson, students will explore their own expertise as readers of body language. They may not realise that they have this skill, or what parts of the body we use in body language but from the 'Getting you thinking' activities, they should quickly realise that they have been using body language to communicate their feelings all their lives.

Getting you thinking

This activity is designed to build some confidence in students in their own use of body language. Some may find it more challenging to produce specific body language when thinking about it, as body language is often an unconscious activity. We may be communicating more than we intend through our body language most of the time!

You may wish to model one or two gestures, facial expressions or movements to get students familiar with the idea before letting them mime their own feelings. Tell them you are listening to some reasons why homework was not handed in; they must decide how you feel about each excuse!

Choose one or two of the pairs to model their mime to the class. Ask the class how they 'knew' how the person performing the mime was feeling. This will lead into 'How does it work?' so you may want to capture their comments about gesture, eye contact, movement, etc. on the board for reference later.

How does it work?

Explain to students that our body language:
- shows how we feel
- can communicate more than 60% of our message
- can change with different people.

Reassure them that we are all very skilful at reading it!

Body language can vary from country to country, for example:
- In Ancient Rome, a 'thumbs up' gesture meant 'life' for the gladiator; in Britain today it means 'OK' or 'Can I have a lift?'!
- Black teenage boys in South Africa often walk to school holding hands. It signifies nothing more than friendship. This gesture would be interpreted differently in the UK.

- In Europe, men and women cross their legs at the knee without any meaning being attached to the gesture. In America, this is seen as not very masculine. A 'masculine' leg cross has the ankle or calf of one leg resting on the knee of the other. (Perhaps you could model this gesture for your class. Is this an acceptable alternative leg cross for boys in class?)

Now you try it

These activities will give students the opportunity to analyse how body language is assembled (face, body gesture) and to interpret what the body language might mean.

Prompt students to:
- describe the body language of the people each time
- decide what the body language might mean.

Take some feedback from the class, and get one or two pairs to talk about how they made their decision.

Ask the class to think about how close people allow others to stand to them when they are talking to them. If you have access to tape measures, students could measure the talking distance between different people.

Talk to students about acceptable body space and about how this varies in different situations.

Interesting findings from a 1966 study can be seen on **http://changingminds.org/ techniques/body/social_distance.htm**

Development activity

Talk to the class about how we hug people differently. You might want to Google 'hugging' for images – there are lots!

Encourage students to think about:
- who we hug
- what happens if we hug for too long or too tightly.

This could be used with just the knowledge they already possess or students could undertake some research. Pairs could make a survey over a week of:
- who they hug and who they don't
- how long their hugs last (quick squeeze or long hug?)

- how tightly they are hugged or hug (gentle or tight squeeze?).

Whichever route you decide on, students can then produce a short piece of writing about how we hug different people differently. This can be assessed for AF4. Success criteria would be that students can write about:

- what hugging is and how it is an example of body language
- how we 'read' body language
- how hugging varies according to participants or place.

Level 5 students should be encouraged to comment on the effect of 'inappropriate' hugging.

Summary

Students have explored different types of body language and had the opportunity to describe and interpret what specific body language might mean.